New Patterns for Bead Flowers and Decorations

by
Virginia Nathanson

Black and white photographs by Rex Nathanson
Color photos by Douglas Corry
Drawings by Barabara Shapira

DOVER PUBLICATIONS, INC
Mineola, New York

Bibliographical Note

This Dover edition, first published in 2004, is an unabridged reprint of the edition originally published by Hearthside Press Incorporated, New York, in 1969. Pages 1 and 2, blank in the original edition, have been omitted in this edition.

Library of Congress Cataloging-in-Publication Data

Nathanson, Virginia..
New patterns for bead flowers and decorations / by Virginia Nathanson ; black and white photographs by Rex Nathanson, color photos by Douglas Corry ; drawings by Barabara Shapira.
p. cm.
Includes index.
Originally published by Hearthside Press, 1969.
ISBN 0-486-43297-1 (pbk.)
1. Bead flowers. I. Title.

TT890.2N39 2004
745058'2—dc22

2003063504

Manufactured in the United States of America
Dover Publications, Inc., 31 East 2nd Street, Mineola, N.Y. 11501

CONTENTS

DEDICATION

Although I know well that dedications are expected to be short and to the point, I must violate the rule this time because it is literally impossible to express my several deep gratitudes in just a few words. The patience of my husband, John, and of my two sons Rex and Brad has been, as usual, far beyond anyone's legitimate expectations.

And the understanding and encouragement of my publishers, Nedda and George Anders, warrant special recognition and thanks. My closest friends and associates must be included as well. All of these are the wonderful people to whom I dedicate this book.

ACKNOWLEDGMENT

Much research has gone into the creating and designing of new patterns for this book, and the actual executing of all the petals, leaves, stamens etc. was extremely time-consuming. I did not carry the burden alone; I could not possibly have done so. This is why I must offer my special thanks to the students whose names follow. Graciously and meticulously, they made the various parts of the majority of flowers included in these arrangements. Without their invaluable assistance, this book might not have appeared for years!

So, my appreciation and gratitude to Mrs. Carolyn Jones, Mrs. Theda Kures, Mrs. Faye Schapiro and Mrs. Maxine Rudman. I offer my additional thanks to the following helpful people who so kindly loaned me their own arrangements for photographic purposes: Mrs. Lillian Seigal, ming tree and petunias; Mrs. Dee Dinkin, tea roses; Mrs. Esther Gross, "birthday cake" arrangement of miniatures; Mrs. Eleanor Scardino, miniature geranium; Mrs. Arline Seide, sweet peas; Mrs. Mildred Bromberg, miniature pink cup and saucer with calla lilies; Mrs. Sue Goldstein, bridal crown.

INTRODUCTION

Because of the tremendous response to, and the success of my first book on beaded flowers, I have been urged and encouraged to write a second one. Of course, all of the original methods and techniques from the first book are included, because these are the nucleus of all bead work. However, the designs and patterns in this volume are new (except for the poinsettias in the Holiday Swag, and the daisies in one of the bridal bouquets). New techniques have been added, also, and once you have mastered them, I am sure you will be able to apply them to many of the flowers in the first book. There are over 90 new patterns for you to try, and 3 new methods on which to test your skills.

It begins with General Instructions followed by Flower Designs, Miniatures, Potted Plants, Holiday Ornaments, and Designs for Brides. There are all sizes and kinds to choose from, and I especially hope the patterns for the little beaded containers will inspire you to attempt different shapes and proportions of your own, once you have learned the method for doing them, as there are so many possibilities.

One of the most exciting hours of each day is mail delivery. I have received literally thousands of letters from coast to coast and around the globe. I try to answer each one personally. Some writers need special help in choosing colors, planning arrangements, and locating proper supplies. Others write just to say "thank you" because they have found a new outlet for their creative abilities. My original offer still stands. Should you need any additional information regarding supplies, interpretation of methods, etc., please feel free to write to me in care of my publishers, enclosing a self-addressed, stamped envelope, and I will gladly answer any of your questions.

A large flower is no more complicated to make than some of the smaller ones. In fact, sometimes they are easier! Try a few of each before planning your arrangements. Read through the general instructions carefully. Become familiar with the terminology used for the various techniques. Then, as you perfect each method, make the flowers that are used in each one. The more you practice, the more perfect your work will be. I have heard from so many of you who have told me of your success in teaching and selling, and it makes me very happy to know that you are not only finding pleasure in working with the flowers, but are bringing so much pleasure to others, which, in itself, is so very rewarding. To those of you who have already added a new "career" to your lives, continued good luck. To those of you who are just starting this fascinating art, I sincerely hope your new hobby brings you a great deal of enjoyment.

I GENERAL INSTRUCTIONS

MATERIALS

Choosing Beads

Your choice of beads, in terms of size, shape and type, is just as important as your color combination.

This book deals entirely with glass beads, and these are manufactured and sold in the following categories: transparent, opaque, lined, processed, and iridescent. Transparent beads are, by definition, clear-colored glass whose permanent color is indeed permanent: it won't fade or wash away. Opaque beads are often referred to as chalk beads; they, of course, are solid and not translucent, and are usually quite brilliant in color. Lined beads are made of clear glass, but have been painted on the inside so as to obtain special color effects you won't find in any other variety of bead. They aren't adversely affected by electric light, but prolonged exposure to sunlight may fade them slightly after a few years' time. Finally, both processed and iridescent beads are permanently colored, with an outside finish that imparts a peculiarly glossy or "rainbow" effect. So much for our bead types.

As to size and shape: the categories are faceted, bugle, and round. Faceted beads, as their name indicates, have been cut into small plane surfaces to give them glitter. Bugle beads, measuring from approximately one-eighth to one-quarter of an inch long, are thin and elongated. You can obtain them in satin finish and in silver, gold, green, blue and red, either silver- or gold-lined, but they aren't used, as a rule, for flower-making; you'll find references to them only in the chapter on holidays, because the bugle beads' tinsel lining tarnishes after constant exposure to air. They serve splendidly for holiday items, which you'll use for only a few weeks each year and then pack away; employed thus, bugle beads will maintain their brilliance indefinitely. However, the *satin* variety used in the lamp designs are white and are, therefore, permanent in color. The round bead is what we'll be dealing with for the most part, because it's the perfect answer to the perfect flower. Round beads are usually uniform in size, and are our best choice for round or pointed petals and leaves.

Beads can be purchased already on the thread. These are the easiest to work with, as it's a simple process to transfer them from thread to wire, which isn't the case with the loose beads sold in packets or small bottles. Threaded beads usually come in bunches containing 12 strands, each of which is approximately 20 inches long.

Interestingly enough, we manufacture no glass beads in the United States. They are all imported, the chief sources being Czechoslovakia, France, Italy, and Japan. As to quality, all are excellent. French beads are noted for their soft, muted subtlety of tone; beads from other countries offer more vibrant and brilliant colors.

How will you identify the color of the beads I refer to in the instructions that follow? Beads are given color *numbers* in their country of origin, like Dior lipsticks—and this is no help to you whatsoever. So in the ensuing pages, when I refer to a color, I'll try to do so descriptively, in the hope that you'll be able to visualize it by association. When I prescribe butterscotch, for example, in Color Plate 10, for the large ti leaves, I literally mean the color of butterscotch candy. Similarly, Wedgwood blue refers to the color of the famous blue china, whereas sapphire blue is the same shade as the gem.

Dye lots can vary, however slightly, from one shipment to the next. Try, when planning a large bouquet or arrangement, to anticipate your bead needs, so that you'll be able to complete the job from a single lot. Any left-overs can be used in the construction of the miniature flowers.

When you buy beads, refer to them not only by color but by size. The size best adapted to general flower-making is 11°; those marked 10° are larger and detract from the delicacy of the petals; size 12° are smaller, and may cause you some difficulty when you try to string them on 28-gauge spool wire. You can buy beads in most hobby and craft shops, and in the needlework department of most large stores.

Selecting Tools and Other Supplies

1. A small wire cutter, with either a side or top cutting surface. You'll need this for cutting heavy stem wires; a small nail clipper will be entirely adequate for cutting spool wire.

2. A small, long-nosed pair of jeweler's pliers. This is really an optional tool, but it makes the twisting of wires considerably easier.

3. Spool wires. You'll want 28-gauge for most petals, leaves, stamens and sepals. 26-gauge, a bit firmer than the 28, is best for larger petals; it makes larger units easier to execute. And for lacing and assembling, you'll use either 30-gauge or 32-gauge.

4. Stem wires. 12-, 14-, or 16-gauge are used to reinforce the larger flowers; 18-gauge for the smaller ones; 19-gauge when you use the large stem beads.

5. Floral tape for assembling. It comes in a wide choice of colors, but those most commonly used are green, light green, twig, brown, and white.

6. Non-hardening modeling clay. This is the best material available for potting your arrangements. Styrofoam just won't hold the weight of most bead flowers.

7. Florist sheet moss. Get it from the florist; it's an excellent covering for the clay. Wood moss, now being used by some florists, is a fairly new product and is most satisfactory. If you decide to bypass moss entirely, you can use small stone chips instead.

8. Containers for the bouquets. Your choice is virtually unlimited. Try glass goblets and bowls which match or harmonize with the beads. Or spray containers with paint that blends or contrasts with the color of your creations. Also, bear in mind that these bead-flower bouquets are bona-fide heirloom pieces: don't hesitate to lodge them in your finest antique china, provided that you first carefully stuff it with modeling clay so as to preclude breakage.

METHODS

First read through and understand the methods given in this chapter. Then string beads onto a spool of wire, following one of the methods given below. After the beads are on wire, you can proceed to make the flowers. Try first one technique and then another. Pointed petals and leaves are the most difficult, so practice some pointed leaves first. If your first points are not too perfect, they won't be noticed in a bouquet, and by the time you have made 15 or 20 of them, they'll be as they should be. Then, making pointed flower petals will seem easy. Don't worry if you are all thumbs: this is typical of all beginners. With practice, you will be able to make every bouquet in the book, no matter how elaborate. Some of the arrangements shown were made by my students, and all of them had the same beginner's problem. This is not an art that one learns in a day or two, but practice will bring perfection.

Keep finished flower parts separated from bunches of beads by putting them in separate envelopes or plastic bags. The end wires of the parts could become entangled in the strands of beads and cause them to become loose.

If you spill beads, the best way to pick them up is to moisten a fingertip, press the finger into the beads, then put the beads onto the wire, one at a time.

After the beads are transferred to a spool of wire you are ready to start. Once you understand the various techniques that are involved, you can become creative and vary the counts and measurements, but follow the original patterns first before experimenting on your own.

The techniques, all described in this chapter and illustrated with step-by-step drawings, are: Basic (Basic Loop, Round Petal, Pointed Leaf), Continuous Single Loops, Continuous Wraparound Loops, Continuous Loopbacks, Continuous Crossover Loops, Shading of Petals, Lacing, Coiled Ends, Single Split Basic, Double Split Basic, Beaded Stems, and Assembly and Use of Floral Tape.

Stringing Beads on Wire

Open a spool of wire. If you are working with a wooden spool, put a thumbtack in the top to anchor the wire so that it won't spiral off. Cut the open end of the wire on the bias (at an angle) to achieve a good point; the beads will go onto the wire much more easily. Loose beads: spill a fair amount into a small saucer or cup, dip the open end of the spool wire into the beads, catching the beads on the wire. Repeat until the required number of beads are strung. Strung beads: gently ease out one end of a strand of beads from the bunch. Insert the open end of the spool wire into the beads, then remove the thread from the beads that are already on the wire. Fig. 1.

Don't take too many beads at a time; an inch or so is plenty. After a little practice, you'll find that the stringing will go very quickly, and that you can accomplish a great deal without even looking. When you've transferred one-half strand of beads to the spool of wire, make a knot at the open end of the string of beads, large enough to prevent the beads from slipping off. Gently remove the opposite end of the strand from the bunch, and continue transferring the remaining beads onto the wire, from the open end of the

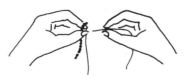

Fig. 1

strand. This will prevent any bead spillage. It is seldom necessary to string more than 2 or 3 strands at a time.

If you run out of beads before finishing a petal or leaf, measure the additional amount of wire needed to finish it by going around the petal or leaf with bare wire for the required number of remaining rows, allowing 3 or 4 inches of extra wire. At this point, cut the wire from the spool. Feed onto the open end of the wire the number of beads needed to finish the petal or leaf. Crimp the open end of the wire after putting them on, so that they won't slip off; now, continue making the unit.

Unless otherwise specified,

Never work with a pre-cut piece of spool wire

Always work directly from the spool

Always complete each petal or leaf before cutting the wire from the spool

Crimp the open end of the spool wire after the required number of beads have been strung on the spool.

Basic Technique

This technique is the one you'll use most frequently for individual leaves and petals. The word "Basic," when followed by a number or measurement, tells you how many beads or inches of beads to put on the center wire, around which the remaining beads are wrapped.

Making the basic loop

Transfer a strand of beads to a spool of wire. Crimp the open end of the wire, move the required number of beads (the basic count) to within 4″ of the crimped end of the wire. Hold your work from underneath so that your hands won't hide it. Place your left thumb and forefinger under the wire and to the right of the basic beads. Then place your right thumb and forefinger under the wire and to the left of the remaining beads on the spool of wire. Fig. 2.

Keep the spool of wire to the right. Have at least 5″ of bare wire between your forefingers. Bring both your forefingers together, as in Fig. 3 and transfer the basic beads and wire to your right thumb and forefinger. With your left hand, twist together the loop of bare wire that is under your right thumb and forefinger. Twist 4 or 5 times very tightly at the bottom of the basic beads, thus closing the loop of wire at the top. Starting on the left side of the basic beads, bring the beaded wire up the left side of the basic beads, wrap

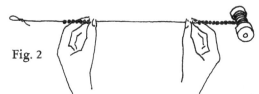

Fig. 2

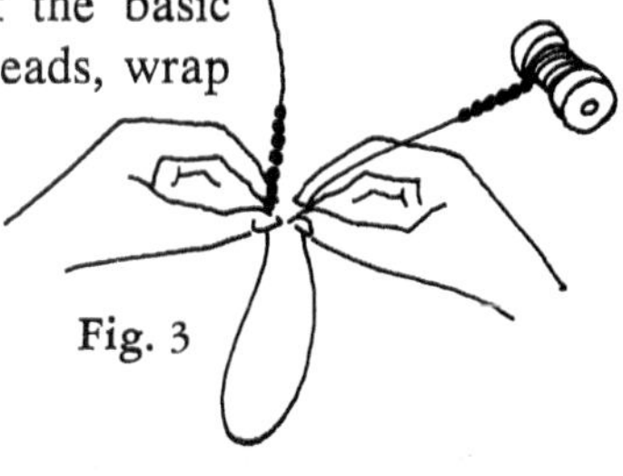

Fig. 3

bare spool wire once around the bare wire at the top of the basic beads—where the single wire is—then come down the right side of the basic beads with beaded wire, and wrap bare spool wire once around the loop wires at the base of the basic beads. Always cross the bare spool wire across the front, to the back, and around to the front again, and wrap firmly. Fig. 4.

Continue wrapping the beaded spool wire around the basic bead row until you have the number of rows called for in your pattern. Keep the rows of beads and the beads themselves close together, and wrap the wires, top and bottom, tightly. The less wire you have showing, the more solid your final effect will be. Your units will be firmer, too. As you work, keep the basic row of beads as straight through the center as possible. Keep the right side of your petals and leaves facing you as you wrap. (After the first few rows have been made, the right and wrong sides will be obvious to you, as more wire shows on the wrong side. To determine the number of rows, count the rows of beads across the center, making sure to include the basic row in your count. The single wire is always considered the top of the petal or leaf, and the loop is the bottom. Always finish at the bottom. This will give you an odd number of rows. There are only a few patterns that call for an even number of rows, in which case you will finish your work at the top of the unit, where the single wire is.

Fig. 4

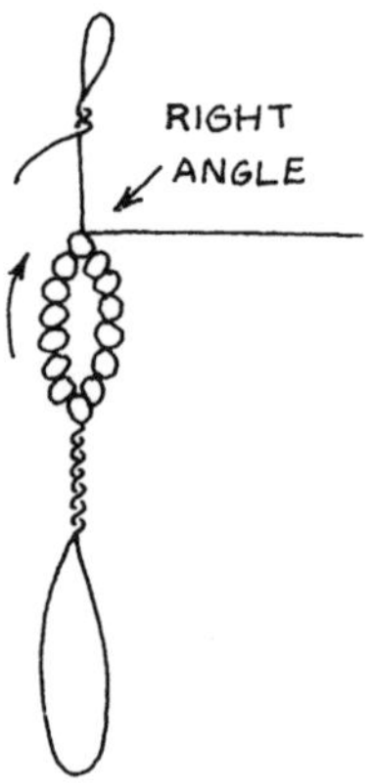

RIGHT ANGLE

Round petals

A beginner usually finds round petals easier to make, so try one, making a basic of 5 beads with 7 rows. As you wrap the bare spool wire around the top and bottom of the basic beads, keep the wire close to the row of beads that precedes it. Each pattern has been figured mathematically to achieve the proper dimension, therefore don't create roundness by bowing out the rows of beads. Keep each new row of beads close to the one next to it. As you make the first wrap at the top of the basic beads, cross in front of the top basic wire, so that the spool wire is horizontal and at right angles to the top basic wire. Wrap the spool wire completely around the top wire, stopping at a right angle position. Fig. 4. Push beads to the top of the basic beads. Turn the petal counter-clockwise (to the left) with the left hand so that the loop is at the top. Wrap bare spool wire around the basic loop, at a right angle, just as you did at the top around the single wire. Fig. 5. Turn your work counter-clockwise again, and repeat, wrapping at the top and at the bottom until the 7 rows of beads have been completed.

As each petal and leaf is finished, cut the top basic wire ¼" from the top, and bend the ¼" of wire down the back of the unit. Tuck it in neatly. Allow 4" of bare spool wire at the bottom of the petal and cut the unit free from the spool of wire. Cut open one side of the basic loop at the base of the petal, then twist the two remaining wires together. Fig. 6.

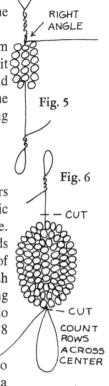

RIGHT ANGLE

Fig. 5

Fig. 6

Pointed petals and leaves

Some petals and leaves have pointed tops and round bottoms; others have round tops and pointed bottoms. Wherever the point, the basic method for making them is the same, except for one slight change. To create a point, go 2 beads beyond the top of the basic beads before wrapping around the bare wire, and change the angle of the spool wire to a 45° angle in relation to the basic wire. Push the beads from the spool wire into the point, and shape it by squeezing the rows of beads together, then flattening the rows so that they do not overlap one another. See Fig. 7 for a pointed top and Fig. 8 for a pointed bottom.

Once the point is started, it must be kept, or the effect is lost, so repeat the procedure each time you work up to the point. For a bottom point, start the point at the end of the third row. For a pointed top, start the point at the end of the second row.

CUT

CUT

COUNT ROWS ACROSS CENTER

Continuous Single Loops

Many flowers are made with continuous loops, each loop worked close to the preceding one. Thistles, wild flowers, asters, tritomas, and peony centers are just a few that are made with the loop method. To make small loops for centers, count the number of beads used for each loop. For larger flower units, the beads are measured. This enables you to work faster and more accurately.

To make a small center consisting of five 10-bead loops, put a few inches of beads onto a spool of wire, crimp the end of the wire, and move 10 beads to within 4" of the crimped end of the wire. Make a loop of the 10 beads by folding them in half and twisting the two wires close to the base of the loop. Twist the wires together, tightly, twice. Close to the base of the first loop, form another 10-bead loop, and give the 10 beads at least one full twist, thus crossing the wires at the bottom of the second loop. It makes no difference

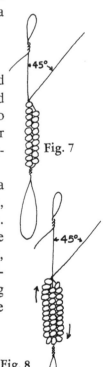

45°

Fig. 7

45°

Fig. 8

whether the twist is toward you or away from you. Just try to be consistent with your directions. Most right-handed people make each new loop to the left of the preceding one, but if it is easier for you to work from left to right, do so, as the end result will be the same. By turning the loops of beads for one full twist, you will be crossing the wires at the base of the loops. Close the base of the second loop, form a third loop with 10 beads, and give this loop a full twist. Make the 4th and 5th loops in the same way. After the 5th loop has been twisted closed, allow 4″ of bare spool wire, and cut the wire from the spool. Twist the 2 wires together under the loops to form a stem, and you have completed a center. Fig. 9.

Fig. 9

Continuous Wraparound Loops

Wraparound petals and leaves are made the same way as the single loops, except that each small loop of beads is encircled with a row of beads around the outside edge, giving it a double row of beads. Let's make the same center as before, but wrap around each loop of beads with a row of beads as we work. String more beads onto the spool of wire, crimp the open end of the beaded spool wire, and move 10 beads to within 4″ of the crimped end of the wire. Make a loop of the 10 beads, then wrap around the outside of this loop of beads with the beaded wire. Wrap bare spool wire around the beginning wire at the base of the wrapped loop of beads. Next to this first wrapped loop of beads, but not quite as close as for making single loops, make another 10-bead loop. Give the loop of beads one full twist, then encircle it with a row of beads. Wrap the bare spool wire around the base of the second loop. Execute the 3rd, 4th, and 5th loops in the same manner, taking care to wrap bare spool wire around the base of each petal after the original 10-bead loop has been encircled with beads. Allow 4″ of bare spool wire at the completion of the last petal, and cut the wire from the spool. Fig. 10. The hydrangea, small red poppy, and primrose are made with continuous wraparound loops.

Fig. 10

Continuous Loopbacks

There are several patterns in which this method is used. It occurs in the leaves of the giant matilija poppy, spider chrysanthemum and spoon chrysanthemums as well as the smaller button and cushion chrysanthemums. The measurements vary, but the principle is the same. To practice, make a small one measuring a 1½″ basic with 5 rows, pointed top, round bottom. Without cutting the beaded wire from the spool, form a loop of beads on the left of this unit, using enough beads to allow the loop to reach from the bottom of the unit to the top of the basic row of beads, and down to the bottom of the unit. Follow the arrows in Fig. 11 for the direction of the beaded wire. At the completion of the first loopback, secure it by wrapping bare spool wire over the front, to the back, and forward between the loopback and the center unit. This will raise the spool wire to its original position at the base of the center 5-row unit. Form a second loopback on the right side of the center 5-row unit, making it the same height as the one on the left, and wrap the spool wire normally, across the front of the bottom basic loop. Make a third loopback on the left and directly under the first one, but shorter. Use just enough beads on the third one to measure halfway up the center unit of 5 rows—to the middle of the basic—cross the spool wire across the front of the bottom basic loop, to the back, and forward between the first and third loopbacks. This will raise the spool wire to its original position again. Form a fourth loopback on the right, and make it the same height as the third one, wrapping the bare spool wire at the bottom normally. Cut open the basic loop at the bottom of the loop, allow 2 or 3 inches of bare spool wire and cut the wire from the spool.

Fig. 11

Continuous Crossover Loops

Flowers made with the crossover method are basically the same as the continuous single loop, except that each loop has a row of beading either up the front and down the back (for a four-row crossover) or a row of beading up the front and bare wire down the back of the loop (for a three-row crossover). The initial loops should be measured for uniformity in size.

String at least 24″ of beads, crimp the open end of the wire, and move 1½″ of beads to within 4″ of the crimped end of the wire. Form the 1½″ of beads into a *narrow* loop, and tightly twist the wires at the base of the loop twice. Bring the beaded wire up the front of the narrowed loop, using just enough beads to fill in the center of the loop. Push the extra beads away, so that the bare spool wire crosses over the top of the loop and goes between the beads at the top of the loop. Bring bare spool wire down the back of the loop, and flatten the petal in the middle so that all three rows of beads are visible. Fig. 12. Wrap bare spool wire around the single

Fig. 12

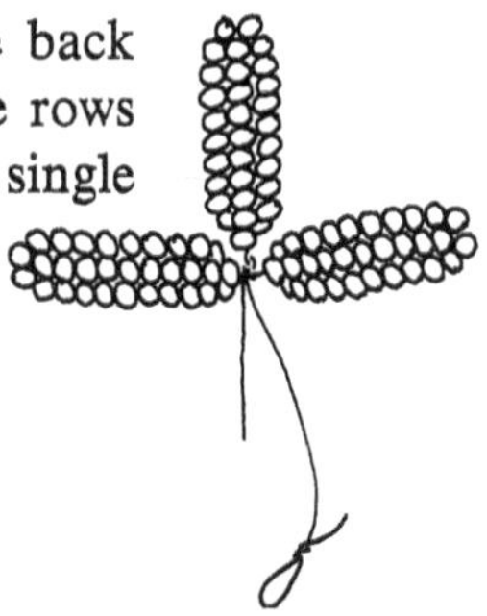

Fig. 12*a*

wire at the base of the petal. You have just made one three-row crossover petal. Close to the base of this first petal, form a loop with another 1½″ of beads, give the loop of beads one full twist to cross the wires at its base, narrow the loop, bead up the front of the narrow loop, cross over the top of the loop with bare wire, bring bare wire down the back of the loop, and wrap bare wire around the base of the second petal to secure the crossover. Repeat for 5 more petals. Allow 4″ of bare spool wire at the completion of the 7th petal, and cut the wire from the spool. Twist the two wires together to form a stem. Make a center for this daisy in a contrast color by using the wraparound method. Make a loop of 8 beads. Wrap around the 8-bead loop with a row of beads, allow 3″ of bare spool wire and cut the wire from the spool. Twist the two wires together, and set the stamen, flat, and in the center of the 7 crossover daisy petals. Twist both sets of wires together to form a stem. Measurements for this little daisy can be increased or decreased as you desire. Change the original loop measurement to 2″, bead up the front and down the back of each petal, and make 9 or 10 petals instead of 7, and you will have made a larger daisy with four-row crossover petals. Increase the count of the stamen to 2 wraparounds instead of only 1, and you have a larger stamen for a larger daisy. The continuous Crossover Loops are used in all of the Chrysanthemum patterns as well as the Stephanotis and Finger Leaves, Fig. 12 *a*.

Shading of Petals

If you wish to shade any of your petals, leave enough bare wire on the petal to completely finish it, as contrast colors must be fed onto the open end of the wire. For example, make a round petal with a 5-bead basic and 7 rows. Work the 5 basic beads and the first 5 rows in the first color. Measure enough bare wire to wrap once more around the petal, measure another 4″ of bare wire and cut the wire from the spool. Feed onto this wire enough beads in a contrast second color to work rows 6 and 7, and finish off the petal. Tipping a petal is done in the same way. Merely change the color of the beads on the top half of the last two rows, finishing off with the original color on the bottom half of the last row. Very attractive effects can be achieved with edging and tipping. Figs. 13 and 14.

Fig. 13

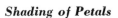

Lacing

Lacing is the method used for reinforcing large petals and leaves.

Fig. 14

One form laces every row together, and the other form skip-laces, as sometimes it is not necessary to lace every row. Lacing is also used to join petals together in a continuous row, as is done in the bud of the giant Matilija poppy bud calyx. To reinforce a single petal or leaf, always start in the middle of the unit. Cut a piece of 30- or 32-gauge assembly wire approximately three times the width of the units that are to be laced. Straddle the middle of the basic row of beads with the assembly wire. Make sure the right side of your work is facing up, unless you are specifically instructed to do otherwise. Cross the assembly wire over one another, on the wrong side of the unit, to lock them in position. You will be back-stitching from the center row to the outside row, working one side of the unit at a time. Keep the top of the unit to the left. Using the piece of assembly wire that is pointed away from you, bring it under the row of beads next to the basic row (the third row), up between the 3rd and 5th rows, across the top of the 3rd row, and down in front of the 3rd row. Bring the wire under the 3rd and 5th rows, up in back of the 5th row, across the top of the 5th row, and down in front of the 5th row; under the 5th and 7th rows, up in back of the 7th row, across the top of the 7th row and down in front of the 7th row, etc. until the outer row has been reached. Lace the outer row also— going around the outer row twice to secure the wire. Clip the excess wire away, very close to the beads. Reverse your work so that the bottom of the units are to the left, still right sides up, and lace the other side of the unit in the same way, bringing the other piece of wire under row 2, up behind row 2, across the top of row 2, down in front of row 2, under rows 2 and 4, up behind row 4, over the top of row 4, down in front of row 4, under rows 4 and 6, up behind row 6, over the top of row 6, down in front of row 6, under rows 6 and 8 etc. until all of the remaining rows have been laced. Wrap the lacing wire twice around the last row to secure, then cut away the excess close to the beads. On some very large petals, such as those for the giant poppy, you can bypass 7 or 8 rows on each side of the basic row, then start your lacing to the outer edge.

When joining petals, one to the other, start the lacing in the middle of the first petal, straddling the basic row of beads, and leave 3″ of the assembly wire pointing away from you. Have the longer end toward you and cross the wires over in the back. The wires will have reversed their position, and the short end will be toward you and the long end will be pointing away from you. Using the longer end

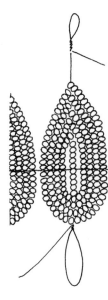

Fig. 15*a*

of the wire, lace to the outside row of the petal, and wrap only once around the last row. Place the second petal close to the first one, making sure that the tops of the petals are even. Bring the lacing wire under, over, and down in front of the first row of beads on the second petal. Continue lacing all the way across the center of the second petal, and add the remaining petals of the flower in the same way, until the required number of petals have been laced together. Turn your work around, still right side up, and finish the lacing for the other half of the first petal, using the short piece of wire. Try to keep the lacing wire in as straight a line as possible. Figs. 15, 15 *a*.

Skip-lacing is used for loop units as in the calyx of the large carnation. For skip-lacing, cut a piece of assembly wire approximately 4 times the width of the unit to be laced. Insert one end of the wire into the first loop, leaving about 2″ of wire extending through the loop. Wrap the longer piece of wire completely around the first loop, bring the wire under loops 1 and 2, over the top of loop 2. Pull the wire toward you. This will draw the first 2 loops close together. Bring the wire down between loops 1 and 2, under loops 2 and 3, up between loops 3 and 4, over the top of loop 3, pull the wire toward you, then bring the wire down between loops 2 and 3. Continue under loops 3 and 4, up between loops 4 and 5, over the front of loop 4, down between loops 3 and 4, under loops 4 and 5, up between loops 5 and 6, etc. until all loops have been wrapped around with the assembly wire. Fig. 16.

Beaded Stems

You may bead a flower stem in two ways. The large flower stems should be wrapped with small beads that have been strung onto a spool of either 30- or 32-gauge wire. However, most medium and small flower stems can be beaded by using large green stem beads.

For wrapped beaded stems, string the small regular 11° green beads onto a spool of assembly wire. String at least 3 strands, as most stems will require that much. After transferring the beads to the spool, wrap the open end of the spool wire around the stem at the base of the flower. Wrap it tightly, 3 or 4 times. Push the beads up to the stem, and wrap them around the stem. Continue wrapping until the desired length has been achieved, then push away

Fig. 15

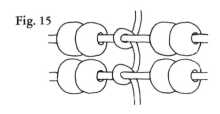

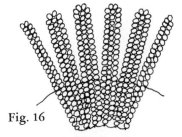

Fig. 16

the beads (toward the spool) and wrap bare spool wire around the stem 3 or 4 times to secure. Cut the wire from the spool, and cover the exposed wire with tape. Fig. 17.

Fig. 17

When using the large stem beads, use 19-gauge wire for the stem of the flower. Always hook the untaped 19-gauge wire into the wires at base of flower to be stemmed. Fig. 18. The hook need not be longer than ½ to ¾ of an inch long. Secure the hook by covering the wires with one width of tape, wrapping the tape 2 or 3 times around. Fig. 19. Cut away all flower wires that extend below the 1 inch of taping at the base of the tape. Cover the tape with small green beads that have been strung on assembly wire. When the bottom of the tape has been reached, wrap bare assembly wire 3 or 4 times around the 19-gauge stem wire, and cut it off very close to the stem. Onto the open end of the stem wire, transfer the desired amount of large stem beads (3, 4 or 5 inches). Turn the stem upside down, cover the bare stem wire with tape, and start the taping from the open end of the stem to the stem beads. Include the 2 top stem beads in the taping. Press the tape firmly and this will prevent the stem beads from slipping and the stem from turning.

Fig. 18

Assembly and Use of Floral Tape

All bare wires at the base of the leaves and all flower stems (not individual petals) should be covered with floral tape before adding leaves and flowers to master-stems. Tape the heavy stem wires, too. Tear 15 or 20 inches of tape from its roll and stretch it as far as possible. Always stretch the tape before using. It will be thinner, and the stems will be slimmer. The tape is slightly adhesive and it has no right or wrong side. Attach one end of the tape to the base of the leaf stems or flower stems, and wrap around and downward at a bias angle. Press as you wrap. Should you need more tape before the wires are covered, simply add another piece of tape to where you left off, and continue. Add leaves to flower stems with more tape. Fig. 20.

Fig. 19

Many of the large flowers are built onto the top of its heavy stem wire and each petal is added with assembly wire. All heavy stem wires, with the exception of the 19-gauge when used for stem beads, are taped before assembly.

Several 6″ rulers have been printed at various locations throughout the book for your convenience. When a pattern calls for a specific measurement, it is important that you measure accurately.

Fig. 20

Stem wires

There are several gauge wires used for flower stems. The 12-gauge is very strong, and should be used for all very large flowers with long stems. A 14-gauge wire is still strong enough to hold a very large flower if the stem is no more than 12 or 14 inches long. A 16-gauge wire holds most large and medium sized flowers if the stems are 10 to 12 inches long. Use 18- or 19-gauge wires for smaller, shorter flowers. If 12-gauge wires are not readily available to you, use two 14-gauge wires taped individually, then taped together side by side. Two or three 16-gauge wires can be combined in the same way for extra strength. Wire clothes-hangers can be straightened with heavy duty pliers and then cut into desired lengths as they have great strength.

Reducing Wires

There is a standard rule for eliminating bottom wires on petals and leaves. Normally, it isn't necessary to reduce them on leaves, as most leaves, when added to flower stems, do show a bit of stem. Therefore, if the basic loop wire is cut open at the bottom of the loop, you will have 3 wires at the base of the leaves: the 2 basic loop wires and the spool wire.

Petal wires should be reduced to 2 wires. To do this safely, cut open one side of the basic loop close to the base of the petal, thus allowing the basic wire to become one wire. The second one is from the spool and should *never* be cut short, as it could cause a petal to come apart during assembly of the flowers if the base wires were twisted the wrong way. Fig. 6.

Split Basic

Because I am constantly trying to find new and better ways to eliminate as many petal wires as possible, the split basic was devised. It eliminates some of the bottom wires, without adding to the danger of a petal opening at the bottom. The end result is a smoother, leaner flower stem.

Single Split Basic

To practice, let's work on a 6-petal daisy with a single split basic. Using a generous basic loop, create a basic of 10 beads, and slip 10 beads more into the basic loop. Fig. 21. Make a 5-row petal

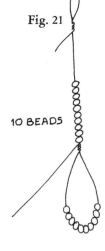

Fig. 21

10 BEADS

10 BEADS

with a pointed top and round bottom, by wrapping the beaded spool wire twice around the top 10 basic beads. If the basic loop wires are twisted below the base of the petal, untwist them back to the base of the petal. Push the 10 beads that are in the basic loop to one side of the loop and cut open the basic loop at the bottom of the loop. Crimp the open end of the side that has the 10 beads. Fig. 22. Wrap the bare spool wire at the base of the 10 beads, and using these 10 beads as another basic, make another 5-row petal with a pointed top and round bottom. Wrap the spool wire twice around the base of the second petal to secure, allow 3″ of bare spool wire and cut the wire from the spool. You will finish with 2 wires: one wire from the spool and one that is the other half of the original basic loop. Trim off the top basic wires normally. This constitutes one pair of petals.

Make 2 more pairs in the same way, stack all 3 pairs, one on top of the other, bottoms even, and twist the bottom wires together to form a stem. Swing the petals into a circle, curving each petal up and out to shape them. You now have only 6 wires in the flower stem instead of the usual 12.

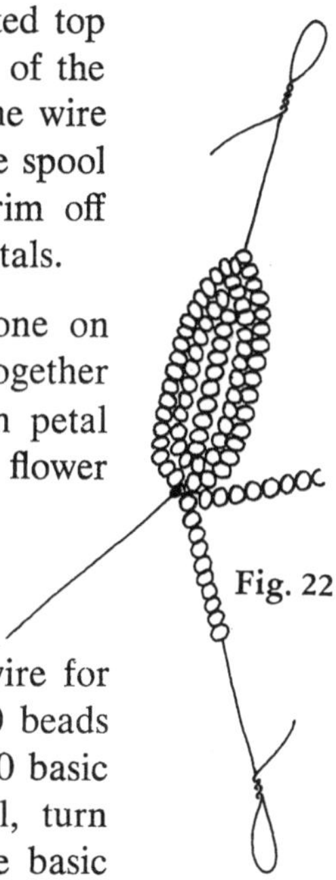

Double Split Basic

The same 6-petal flower can be made with 1 remaining wire for each 3 petals. Create the same basic of 10 beads, and slip 20 beads into a generous basic loop. Make a 5-row petal with the top 10 basic beads, untwist the basic loop back to the base of the petal, turn the petal upside down, and put 10 beads on each side of the basic loop. Fig. 23. Cut open the basic loop in the middle of the loop, crimp both open ends of the wires to prevent the beads from slipping off, wrap bare spool wire twice around the bottom of the 10 basic beads on the left wire, and make a 5-row petal, pointed top, round bottom. Wrap bare spool wire around the base of the 10 beads on the right wire, and make a third 5-row petal. At the completion of the 5th row on the last petal, wrap bare spool wire, twice, around the base of the third petal. Allow 3 or 4 inches of bare spool wire and cut the wire from the spool. You now have 3 petals and one wire. Make another set of 3 petals in the same way, stack them, bottoms even, right sides up, and twist the 2 bottom wires together to form a stem. Shape the petals into a flower.

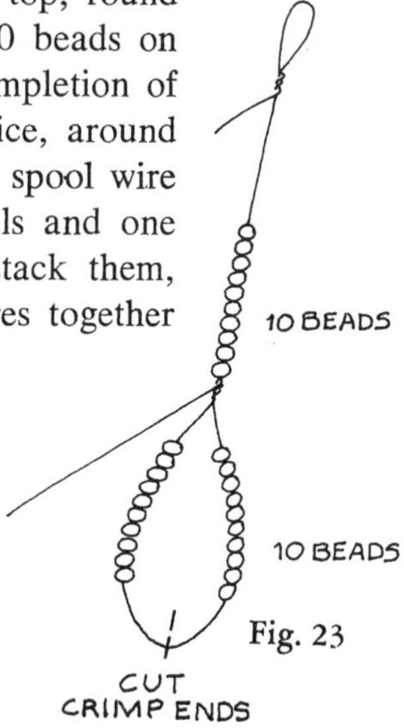

Fig. 22

10 BEADS

10 BEADS

Fig. 23

CUT
CRIMP ENDS

Flowers with more than 5 rows of beads can be made the same way, but more than 2 wraps of the spool wire will be necessary at the start of each new petal so that there will be enough space between the base of the first completed petal and the base of each new petal. You must allow enough space for the rows of beads on each new petal. The space should be equal to the distance between the bottom basic bead of the first petal to the bottom of the bottom row of the first petal. Figs. 24, 25.

To make a 5-petal flower, work one pair of petals with a single split basic, and a trio of petals with a double split basic. You will have only 3 bottom wires for the 5 petals. Combine these petals in the same way as before.

Reverse Wrap

Often, a reverse wrap can give your petals and leaves a neater appearance. For example, the outside petals of the tea rose are reverse-wrapped. Because the top of the petals are rolled back, the wire on the wrong side doesn't show. However, unless the sepals are pressed upward and close to the base of the rose, the wrong side at the bottom of the petals will show a great deal of wire; therefore, at the completion of every odd-numbered row (3, 5, 7, etc.) cross the bare spool wire *under,* over and around the bottom basic loop. This will give your petal a right side at the top and a wrong side at the bottom. On the other side, you will have just the reverse: a wrong-sided top and a right-sided bottom. When adding the outer petals, attach them with the right side of the bottom of the petal on the outside. Whenever a reverse wrap is requested in a pattern, execute it at the round end of the unit, as it is easier, and you will not risk

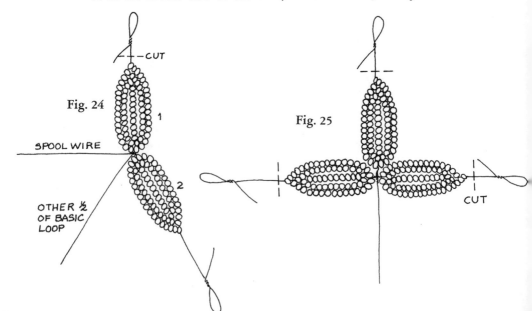

Fig. 24

SPOOL WIRE

OTHER ½
OF BASIC
LOOP

Fig. 25

CUT

spoiling your point at the other end. If the pattern calls for a round top *and* bottom then it makes no difference which end you reverse wrap.

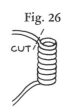

Fig. 26

Coiled ends

There are several designs that call for coiled ends at the open ends of the wires. The stamens in the Meadow Rue and the large units of the Spider Chrysanthemum are just 2 examples. The coiled end of the wire can be made with either a sharp-nosed jeweler's pliers by bending back the extreme tip end of the wire and giving it one complete turn to close the small loop, or with a darning needle or corsage pin. Wrap the wire around the pointed end of the needle 2 or 3 times and push the coils close together. Remove the needle or pin from the coiled wire and cut away the very tip end, which was not coiled. Fig. 26.

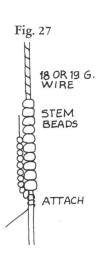

Fig. 27

Reinforcing Extra-Large Leaves

There are 2 shortcuts to making very large leaves more easily. The first is to use large green stem beads for the basic of a large leaf. The very long leaf for the giant iris was made this way. Cut a 12″ piece of 19- or 20-gauge wire and tape one end for 3″. Onto the opposite end slip 7″ of stem beads, and tape the remaining stem wire at the top so that the beads are tightly set between the two tapings. Using 26-gauge spool wire strung with regular green beads, attach the open end of the bare spool wire at the base of the stem beads. Wrap it 3 or 4 times, then build the leaf, normally, wrapping beads around the stem beads, until the required number of rows have been completed. Fig. 27.

It is also possible to make a long leaf without having any basic row of beads in the middle. Cover a generous piece of 18- or 19-gauge wire with tape, attach the beaded spool wire 2 or 3 inches up from one end and use 2 inches of beads on the first row of beads. Wrap bare spool wire around the heavy wire, and bead down the other side. Continue wrapping with beaded wire until the desired number of rows have been completed, creating either round or pointed tops. When the leaf is finished you will have an even number of rows of beads because there is no basic row. Press the rows of beads together, especially in the center to hide the heavy wire that is down the middle. Lace once through the middle of the leaf if it is necessary. Fig. 28.

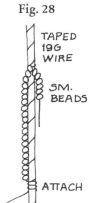

Fig. 28

Silking the Stems

You have no doubt noticed the absence of any instructions for using silk floss on the stems of the flowers. This is essentially because I object to the fact that the floss most readily obtainable, unfortunately, does not match the colors of the beads that we use for the leaves. If it did, I would use it more often. Should you be fortunate enough to have floss that blends well with the shade of green you are using, by all means floss the stems. It's a rather simple process: Start the thread at the base of the flower, allowing an inch or so to extend down the stem. Wrap the thread down and around the stem and include the inch in the wrapping. Wrap the threads close together so that there is no exposed wire. When the desired length has been completed, cut off the thread and secure the end with either a small piece of masking tape or Scotch tape. Add leaves to the stem as you wrap if you wish. Take care when washing the flowers, as the thread is silk and will lose its sheen if it isn't rinsed well.

II FLOWER DESIGNS

5" x 3". See also color plate 7.

ANTHURIUM (Arum)

One of the most spectacular flowers in the Arum group, the Anthurium spathe is large, bold, and particularly exotic. It is usually bright red or orange, and the stems are strong and erect.

Materials for one

Beads: 4½ strands for spathe; 1 strand yellow for stamen
Wires: 26-gauge spool; 14- or 16-gauge for stem

Spathe

Basic: 6 beads, pointed top, round bottom, 36 rows. Make 1.

Transfer at least 4½ strands of beads to the spool wire before starting the spathe. Working with a generous basic loop (12") and top basic wire (6"), create a basic of 6 beads, also using 6 beads for row 2. Wrap spool wire twice at the finish of the second row to secure it, and insert a pencil between the 2 rows of beads to shape the 2 rows of beads into a circle. Work for 10 rows, keeping the petal round at both ends. Fig. 29. At the completion of row 10, cut open the bottom of the basic loop. This will give the petal 2 bottom basic wires. Make row 11 and secure it by wrapping 1½ times around the bottom wire on the right. This will reverse the direction. Bead up to the top basic wire, wrap normally, but start a one bead point. Bead down the left side of the petal and wrap 1½ times around the bottom basic wire on the left. This will reverse the direction. Bead up the left side and wrap normally around the top basic wire, and continue with the 1 bead point. Bead down to the wire on the right side, wrap 1½ times, bead up to the top, and down the left side and wrap 1½ times, etc. until 36 rows have been completed. Keep

Fig. 29

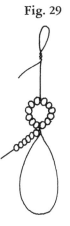

Fig. 30

the 1 bead point at the top, guard against making the split at the bottom of the petal too wide. Keep it close together for the first few rows, then widen it out slightly. You will finish at the top of the petal. Allow 2″ of spool wire and cut the wire from the spool. Twist together, tightly, the two top wires, cut away all but ¼″ and flatten it down the wrong side of the petal. Top dress the bottom split of the petal by feeding onto both wires enough beads to cover the top of both sides with beads. Fig. 30. Push the wires through to the back of the petal and twist them together. Lace the petal in 3 places, once through the middle, half way down from the top to the center lacing, and half way up from the bottom of the petal to the center lacing. Lace with the right side of the petal facing up.

Stamen

Two inches from the crimped end of the spool wire, make a narrow loop of 5″ of beads, bead up the front and down the back of the beaded loop, the same as for any crossover petal. Wrap bare spool wire around the bottom wire, and cross over once more by beading up the front and down the back, giving the stamen 6 rows of beads in all. Secure at the bottom by twisting both wires together. Insert the stem of the stamen into the open circle in the center of the petal. Twist both sets of wires together, and cover them with tape. Tape a heavy stem wire, cut to the desired length, and tape the flower stem and the stem wire together. Start the heavy stem wire close to the base of the petal. Wrap the stem with green beads strung on 30- or 32-gauge wire, if desired.

Flower, 1½″ in diameter.
Spray, 4″ x 2½″.
See also color plate 19.

ASTER (*Novae angliae*)

An adaptation of the small asters that grow in wild profusion throughout New England, it comes in a wide range of pastels, and lends itself well to a bouquet of small spring flowers, yet it has enough charm of its own to be used alone.

Materials for one sprig (2 flowers, 1 bud, 3 leaves)

Beads: 2 strands for flowers and bud; 3" yellow for flower centers; 1 strand green for leaves and bud calyx
Wires: 28-gauge silver or 26-gauge gold spool; 18-gauge for stem

Flower

Make 2, in any pastel color or white. Make 10 continuous loops, measuring 1½" of beads for each loop.

Centers: 1 for each flower in yellow. Make an 8-bead loop and wrap around it once with a row of beads.

Assembly of Flower

Slide the wires of one center in between any pair of loops and twist both sets of wires together for ½" under the flower to form a stem. Press the center flat. Tape both sets of wires with ½-width tape.

Bud

(Same color as flower. Make 1.) Make 4 continuous loops, measuring 1" of beads for each loop.

Bud Calyx

In green; make 1 for each bud. Make 2 continuous loops counting 10 beads for each loop.

Assembly of Bud

Set the bud loops in between the 2 green calyx loops and press the green loops flat against the base of the bud loops. Twist both sets of wires together to form a stem, and cover with ½-width tape.

Leaves

Make a narrow loop with 4" of beads. Give the narrow loop of beads 2 more rows of beads by beading up the front and down the back of the initial loop. Twist bottom wires together and tape with ½-width tape. Make 3, in green.

```
        1           2           3           4           5
 └───┴────┴────┴────┴────┴────┴────┴────┴────┴────┘
```

Assembly of Sprig

Using ½-width tape, cover a 7- or 8-inch piece of 18-gauge wire and add it to one flower 1¼" below the base of the flower. Tape down the stem for ½" and add 1 leaf on the left (no stem showing on the leaves). One-half inch lower, on the right, add another leaf. One-half inch lower, add the bud to the left, and the second flower to the right. Allow 1½" of stem on the bud and the 2nd flower, then add the 3rd leaf.

Flower, 2" in diameter.
Leaf, 3" long.
See also color plate 11.

BACHELOR BUTTONS (*cornflowers*)

These lacy flowers are usually a deep, bright blue, but they also grow in pale pink and white. They are shown with 2 finger leaves rather than their natural thin spike leaves which aren't too attractive. However, if you prefer, add 2 pair of Basic 3" 3 rows, pointed tops and round bottoms to each of the flowers instead of the finger leaves.

Materials for one flower, two finger leaves

Beads: 6 strands for flower, 4½ strands green for leaves and calyx; stem beads are optional.
Wires: 26- or 28-gauge spool; 16- or 19-gauge for stem

Flower

Unit 1. Make 10 continuous loops, measuring 1" of beads for each loop. Balance the wires, twist them together, narrow the loops, and cup them to the center. Make 1 for each flower, in blue.
Unit 2. Crimp the open end of the beaded spool wire and push ¾" of beads to the crimped end of the wire. Three inches from the crimped end of the wire, make 3 continuous 10-bead loops. Push the ¾" of beads to the base of the first loop of beads, bring beaded

wire to the bottom of the ¾″ of beads, and wrap bare spool wire around the bare wire at the bottom of the first ¾″ of beads. Fig. 31. Bring beaded wire up the left side of the 2 rows of beads, force bare spool wire between the 2nd and 3rd beaded loop, from front to back, cross the bare wire to the left of the 3rd beaded loop. Make 2 more 10-bead loops to the left of the 3rd loop, bead down to the bottom of the petal and twist the bottom wires together. Fig. 32. Make 7 for each flower in blue.

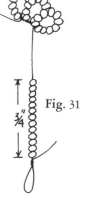

Fig. 31

Calyx (*green*)

Make 7 continuous loops, measuring 1″ of beads for each loop. Make 1 for each flower.

Assembly of Flower

For taped stem: mount Unit 1 to the top of a 16- or 19-gauge stem wire and tape for 1½″. Cut away the excess wires from Unit 1 at the base of the tape. Attach a 15″ piece of 30- or 32-gauge wire to the base of Unit 1 and add the 7 petals of Unit 2 around the base of Unit 1. Add the calyx around the base of the flower, thin out the petal and calyx wires and cover with tape.

Tape on 1 or 2 finger leaves 3½″ below the base of the flower, one on the left and one on the right.

For beaded stem: Twist together the wires of Unit 1 and hook a 19-gauge stem wire into the base of the unit. Tape for 1″. Add the 7 petals of Unit 2 and calyx with lacing wire, tape for 1″, trim away all wires from the flower parts at the base of the taping, and proceed as described in General Instructions for Beaded Stems.

Fig. 32

Flower head, 4″ x 5″.
With stem and leaves, 15″ long.
See also color plate 7.

BIRD OF PARADISE (Strelitzia)

This gorgeous and unusual flower is perhaps the strangest of all tropical flowers, for it strongly suggests the head of a bird. Several blossoms are packed tightly into a long green pod, and as they emerge, the cluster becomes larger. For practical reasons, there are only 2 blossoms shown in this pattern. Each blossom has 3 pointed petals in bright orange, and a stamen in sapphire blue.

Materials for one flower

Beads: 2½ strands blue; ½ bunch orange; 1 bunch dark green
Wires: 26-gauge spool; one 14-gauge or two 16-gauge spools for stem

Flower

Unit 1. BASIC: 1¼″, pointed top, round bottom, 13 rows. Make one, in orange.
Unit 2. BASIC: 2¼″, pointed top, round bottom, 11 rows. Make two, in orange.
Reduce to two the bottom wires of both units.

Stamen

This unit is made all in one (continuously) without cutting the wire from the spool until it is completed. Create a basic with 2¼″ beads, with 4½″ of beads in the basic loop. Add 3 rows of beads to the 2¼″ basic (making four rows in all) pointed top, and round bottom. You will finish at the top. Create a narrow loopback, down the right side of the 4 rows of beads, and use 3¼″ of beads for the loopback. Cross the spool wire over the top basic wire, swing it to the back and bring it forward between the loopback and the center unit of 4 rows of beads. This will raise the spool wire to its original position at the base of the 4 rows of beads. Using another 3¼″ of beads, create another narrow loopback on the left and secure it by wrapping the

34

spool wire normally. Twist the spool wire and the top basic wire together for ½″, cut off all but ¼″ and press it flat against the wrong side of the beading. Fig. 33.

Turn the stamen upside down, and divide the 4½″ of beads that are entrapped in the basic loop, so that there are 2¼″ of beads on each side of the basic loop. Cut open the basic loop at the bottom of the loop and crimp both open ends. With each wire make a narrow beaded loop in each side of the center 4 rows of beads, twist the 2 wires together to form a stem and cut off the crimped ends. Fig. 34. Make 1, in blue.

Leaves

Large for pod. BASIC: 2½″, pointed top and bottom, 17 rows. Lace in 3 places with the right side up. If dark green wire in 30- or 28-gauge is available to you, use it for the lacing as it will be less obvious against the dark green beads. Leave the 6 ends of the lacing wires for closing the pod during assembly. Cover the bottom wires with tape. Make 1 in dark green.

Small. BASIC: 2″, pointed top, round bottom, 15 rows. Make 2 in dark green. Lace each leaf in two places, right sides up, lock in the lacing wires between the last 2 rows of beads on each side, and cut off the excess wire close to the beads. Cover the bottom wires with tape.

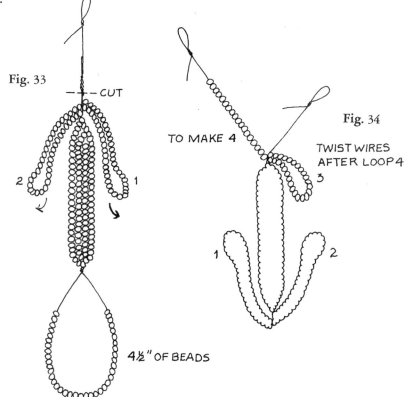

Fig. 33

CUT

2   1

4½″ OF BEADS

TO MAKE 4

Fig. 34

TWIST WIRES
AFTER LOOP 4

3

1   2

Assembly of Blossom

Stack the petals and stamen in the following order; with the right sides facing up; one Unit 2, one stamen, one Unit 2, then one Unit 1 with the wrong side up. Twist the bottom wires together and cover with tape. Swing the Unit 1 petal to the left and cup it upward. Swing the stamen toward the left, and the two Unit 2 petals to the right bowing them slightly. Repeat for the second blossom.

Assembly of Flower

Tape a 12″ or 14″ cut of 14-gauge wire or two 16-gauge wires taped together, side by side. The flower is heavy and needs the support of a heavy stem. Bend the top 3½″ of the stem wire at an angle. Tape on the first flower one and a third inches from the end of the stem wire. Tape for 1″ and add the second flower. Fold the large pod in half lengthwise, and set the flowers in the center. Tape the pod stem to the flower stem, and join the lacing wires at the top side of the pod by twisting each pair together for ½″ then cutting away all but ¼″ of the twisted wire. Fig. 35. Tuck this ¼″ of wire inside the pod.

Starting at the base of the pod, wrap the stem for 3¼″ using the dark green beads strung on 30- or 32-gauge lacing wire. At the completion of the 3¼″ of beading, tape on 1 small leaf, continue beading the stem, either for 3¼″ and adding a second leaf, or bead down the stem for 6″, depending on your arrangement and the amount of greenery you want to use.

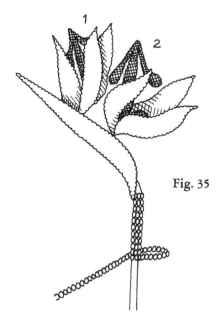

Fig. 35

11″ x 4″. See also color plate 19.

BITTERSWEET (*Celastrus scandens*)

A very ornamental flower in dried arrangements, the small green leaves of the bittersweet turn yellow in the Fall and burst open to reveal a bright orange seed pod.

Materials for one branch (18 flowers)

Beads: 4 strands dark yellow or mustard for petals; 1½ strands dark orange or bittersweet for berry

Wires: 28-gauge silver or 26-gauge gold spool; 18- or 19-gauge for stem

Tape: Brown or twig for assembly

Each flower has a dark orange berry in the center of 4 dark yellow petals. In the arrangement on Color Plate 19 there are 100 of the flowers attached to stem wires, and they are in groups of 4 and 5 flowers.

Berry

Two and one-half inches from the crimped end of the spool wire make a loop of 12 orange beads, and close the loop of beads by giving it 3 half twists. Bring beaded wire up the front and down the back of the loop to form a 4-row crossover loop. Twist the 2 end wires together for ½″ to form a stem. Make one for each flower, in orange.

Petals

These petals in dark yellow or mustard are made in pairs with a single split basic technique, and each flower requires 2 pairs. Make one pair by creating a 3-bead basic and 3 rows, pointed top, round bottom, and wrap bare spool wire around the base of the petal twice, to secure. Cut open the basic loop at the bottom of the loop. Onto one of these wires put 3 beads, thus creating another basic of 3

37

beads. Bead once around this second basic, giving it 3 rows in all, with a pointed top and round bottom. Repeat, making another pair in the same way.

Assembly of Flower

Set 1 pair of petals on top of the other pair, right sides facing, bottoms even, and twist together both sets of wires for ½". Open the petals into a circle, set an orange berry in the center of the 4 petals and twist together all of the wires to form a stem. Cover the wires with half-width brown or twig tape. Group the bittersweet in clusters of 4 or 5 flowers, and add them to taped 18- or 19-gauge stem wires, to form twigs. Combine 2 or 3 twigs to form branches.

Leaf, 5½" x 2".
See also color plate 14.

BOSTON FERN

This is the fern that was my grandmother's pride and joy. She had a "green thumb" with these and the front parlor displayed several healthy plants. Shown in a lavabo in Plate 14, they will brighten any corner of a room, or you may use them as fillers at the base of a large arrangement. The pattern that follows is meant to be a guide, and the count can be increased or decreased in size, to comply with your individual needs. Use the ferns singly or in groups of threes.

Materials for one fern leaf

Beads: 5 strands
Wires: 26-gauge spool; 18- or 19-gauge for stem
   Tape a 12" piece of 18- or 19-gauge stem wire with ½-width tape. Three inches from one end of the stem wire, attach the open end of the beaded spool wire. Form a narrow 2" loop of beads to the right side of this stem wire, cross bare spool wire once around the stem wire to secure the loop. The direction of the loop should be

1   2   3   4

from bottom to top. Follow the arrows in Fig. 36. Form a 2nd
narrow 2" beaded loop directly opposite the 1st loop on the left, but
this time the direction of the loop should be from top to bottom.
Cross bare spool wire over the top of the stem wire at the base of
the 1st and 2nd loops, bring bare spool wire under the stem wire,
to the left, and over the top of the stem wire at the top of the base
of the 1st and 2nd loops. The spool wire should now be on the right
side of the stem wire again, in position to create a 3rd 2" beaded
loop directly above loop 1. Form a 3rd beaded loop on the right,
working from bottom to top, wrapping bare spool wire over the top,
once, and around the stem wire. Form the 4th 2" beaded loop
directly opposite the 3rd loop, from top to bottom. Bring bare spool
wire over the top of the stem wire, in between loops 1 and 2, under
the stem wire to the left, over the top and to the right above loop 3.
All loops made on the right side of the stem wire are made from down
to up, and the wrapping of the spool wire is once around, normally.
All loops made on the left side of the stem wire are made from up
to down, and the spool wire wraps over the top, under, to the left,
and over the top to the right.

Pattern

Make twelve 2" loops, 6 on each side
Make six 2" loops, less 2 beads, 3 on each side
Make six 1¾" loops, 3 on each side
Make six 1½" loops, 3 on each side
Make six 1¼" loops, 3 on each side
Make 10 1" loops, 5 on each side, and make one 10-bead loop for
the top. Bring beaded wire down the center of the front, securing it
every 1½" to 2" by wrapping bare spool wire between a pair of
loops and around the stem wire. At the bottom, when the center
beaded vein has been completed, wrap bare spool wire around the
stem wire 2 or 3 times to secure, cut away the spool wire and cover
the bare wires with tape. Be sure to keep all of the loops narrow
and close together. Cut away all but ½" of the top of the stem
wire, and turn it down the wrong side of the fern.

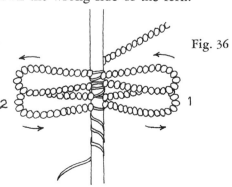

Fig. 36

9½'' x 6½''. See also color plate 1.

BOUDOIR LAMPS

The petals for the small lamps are the same size as those used in the console lamps. There are 32 petals around the frame of each lamp and each lamp has 4 flowers with 10 petals each. The center units are continuous loops with one pearl teardrop in the center. Almost any center will be attractive. Experiment with several unusual kinds of beads until you find one you like. Make a large unit of the primrose, for example, or perhaps three 12-bead loops surrounded with 3 round petals, using a 5-bead basic and 5 rows.

Materials

Beads: 3 bunches for petals
Wires: 26- or 28-gauge spool; 14-gauge for frame

Each frame uses 2 pieces of 14-gauge wire 13'' long and shaped as in Fig. 37. The petals are taped around the outside edge of the frame ½'' apart and the flowers are taped to the combined center wires of the frame, the same as for the large lamps. These frames are mounted on small French antique brass candlesticks, then electrified.

Fig. 37

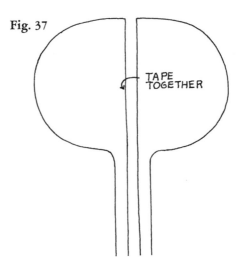

TAPE
TOGETHER

Spray, 9″ long.
See also color plates 11, 17.

BRIDAL WREATH (Spirea)

One of the first shrubs to blossom in early summer is this plant with its soft and lacy flowers. They can add line and grace to any arrangement, and when made in beads, are guaranteed not to "shed"! See bridal wreath in Color Plate 11 combined with red peonies and blue cornflowers.

Materials for one spray

Beads: 1 bunch white; ½ bunch light green; 1 strand yellow for centers

Wires: 26-gauge gold for flowers; 26- or 28-gauge silver for leaves; 24-gauge for stemming flower clusters; 16-gauge for stem

Each branch of spirea is made of clusters of flowers. Each cluster has 12 flowers and 4 leaves. The branch can be as long or as short as you wish it, depending on how it is to be used in a bouquet. The one shown has 9 clusters.

Flower

Three inches from the open end of the spool wire, make 4 continuous 7 bead loops. Allow 3″ of bare spool wire and cut the wire from the spool. Cross the wire at the base of the 4th loop under the 1st loop and bring it up between the 1st and 2nd loops. Put 1 yellow bead onto the wire, push the bead to the bottom of the wire, cross the wire over the top of the flower and bring it down between the 3rd and 4th loops. This will secure the 1 yellow bead in the center of the flower. Twist both wires together at the underside of the flower for at least 1½″, to form a stem. Make 12 for each cluster. Make 108, in white.

Leaf

Basic: 5 beads, pointed tops, round bottoms, 5 rows.

Reduce the bottom wires to 2, and tape the wires together with

41

½-width tape. Make 48 (4 for each 12 flowers) in green.

Assembly of Flower Cluster

Cover a 4″ piece of 24-gauge wire with ½-width tape. Still using ½-width tape, add 12 flowers, one at a time, to the top of the stem wire. Allow no more than 1″ of stem on each flower. Thin out the flower stem wires at odd lengths, so that the cluster stem remains as thin as possible, and tape on 4 leaves at 1/3″ intervals, down the stem. Place 2 on the left and 2 on the right of the stem.

Assembly of Branch

Use full width tape and cover a 12″ piece of 16-gauge wire, and to the top of it tape on a cluster of flowers, attaching the top of the heavy stem at the base of the lowest leaf on the cluster. Tape down the stem wire for 1″ and tape on a second cluster of flowers on the left side of the 16-gauge wire. Tape down another 1″ and add another cluster on the right side of the 16-gauge wire. Space all clusters one inch apart, alternating sides, until the desired number of clusters have been added. If extra long branches are desired, reinforce with another piece of 16-gauge wire and tape it to the first wire, starting at the base of the last cluster, then continue adding more clusters, spacing them 1″ apart.

10″ x 8½″.

BUTTERFLY TIEBACKS

Drapery tiebacks can be created from any number of patterns, but the giant butterfly is one of the most unusual. This large one is mounted firmly to the top surface of a plastic tieback that is readily obtainable in any drapery department. The pattern calls for 3 colors, black, yellow, and white, but any 3 colors may be used, or it can be just as attractive in one color.

Materials for one

Beads: 2 strands black; 3 strands yellow; 15 strands white
Wires: 26-gauge spool; 30- or 32-gauge lacing; 19-, 20-, 22-, or
  24-gauge stem for bracing wings

Wings

Large. BASIC: 10 beads, pointed top, round bottom, 33 rows. Make 2.

Work with a long basic loop—at least 12″ (6″ when folded) and a generous top basic wire—at least 8″. Make one large wing with the basic wire curved to the right, and the other one with the basic wire curved to the left. String black beads first and work the first 9 rows (basic row included) in black. Allow 30″ of bare spool wire and cut the wire from the spool. Feed on enough yellow beads (about 24″) to make the next 8 rows (10, 11, 12, 13, 14, 15, 16, and 17, 4 on each side). Allow 6″ of bare spool wire and cut off the excess. Onto the spool wire transfer at least 5 strands of white beads. Attach the open end of the spool wire to the base of the wing and continue building the large wing by adding 16 rows of white beads (8 on each side). Allow 6″ of bare spool wire and cut the wire from the spool. Remove all but 1½″ of the top basic wire and cover it with tape. Tape a 10″ piece of lightweight stem wire (19-, 20-, 22-, or 24-gauge) and tape it to the 1½″ of taped top basic wire, making an extended top basic wire for extra firmness. Bring the stem wire down the back of the wing and tape it to the bottom wires of the wing. Lace across the wing in 2 places, with the right side facing up, and include the bracing wire as you lace. Start the first lacing at the bottom of the basic row of beads, and the second lacing at the top of the basic row of beads. If you find the wing easier to make by lacing as you work, complete the first 9 rows, then start the lacing at the bottom of the basic row, work 2 rows and lace, work 2 more rows and lace, etc. until you have completed all 33 rows. Lock in the lacing wires and cut off the excess close to the beads on the wrong side of the wing.

Small. Make 2. One small wing with the basic curved to the right and a second wing with the basic wire curving to the left. Lace and brace the same as for the large wings, following the same pattern but reduce the number of black rows from 9 to 7, the number of yellow rows from 8 to 6, and the number of white rows from 16 to 12.

Body

BASIC: 4″, pointed top, round bottom, 11 rows.

Brace the body down the back the same as for the wings, and lace, once through the middle, right side facing up, and include the bracing wire in the lacing. Tape the bracing and bottom wires together, lock in the lacing wire ends and cut off the excess close to the beads on the wrong side of the body. Make 1, in white.

Antennae

Three inches from the open end of the beaded spool wire make a narrow loop of 8″ of beads. Give the narrow loop a 4-row crossover by beading up the front and down the back of the loop. Twist the bottom wires together for 3″ and cut the wire from the spool. Repeat and combine the bottom wires of the 2 loops by twisting them together and taping them. Spiral each 4-row crossover loop, tightly. Make 2, in white.

Assembly of Butterfly

Combine one pair of wings by setting the small right-curved wing on top of the large right-curved wing, bottoms even. Tape the bottom wires together. Combine the 2 left-curved wings in the same way. Put both pair together, right sides facing each other (in) and bottoms even. Tape both sets of wires together and spread the wings open, right sides up. Combine the bottom wires of the body and antennae by taping them together. Place the combined body and antennae wires between the 2 pairs of wings so that the body is partly over the pair of small wings, and the antennae are forward, between the 2 large wings.

With wire and masking tape, firmly attach the butterfly stem wires to a plastic tieback, and cut away any excess stem wires. Top dress the masking tape and wires with either floral tape, satin ribbon or matching fabric.

1   2   3   4

Flower, 6" x 2¾".
See also color plate 2.

CALLA LILY (*Zantedeschia aethiopica*)

The calla lily is a most regal flower. The sculptural quality of its chiseled blossom and majestic leaves is such that it is seen to best advantage apart from other flowers. The large spathe is the color of cream and the stamen (spadix) is pale-to-deep yellow. These are varieties of callas in pale pink and yellow, but the white ones are easily the most spectacular.

Materials

Beads: 8 strands white (pearl or alabaster); 14" yellow for stamen; 8 strands green for leaf

Wires: 26- or 28-gauge spool; 30- or 32-gauge lacing; 14- or 16- gauge for stems

Petal

Basic: 5 beads, pointed top, round bottom, 39 rows. Make 1 for each lily.

Have at least 8 strands on the spool wire before starting. Work with a very long basic loop and top basic wire (12" in the loop and 6" at the top). After working 10 or 11 rows, start lacing in two places, with the right side of the petal facing up. With one piece of lacing wire, lace across the petal starting at the top of the basic row. With the 2nd piece, start the lacing at the bottom of the basic row. Lace together the rows that have already been made, then lace each row as it is made until 39 rows have been completed. Lock in the lacing wires, and cut the excess wires away, close to the beads. (See General Instructions Chapter, Lacing Individual Petals and Leaves.)

Stamen (spadix)

Create a narrow loop with 7" of beads. Close the wires at the bottom of the loop by twisting them twice, tightly, close to the base of the beads. Bring beaded wire up the front and down the back of the beaded loop, giving the original loop of 7″ of beads (3½″ when made into a loop) a 4-row crossover. Twist the bottom wires together for 2″ and cut away the spool wire. Spiral the crossover loop by twisting all four rows of beads together. Make 1 for each flower, in yellow.

Assembly

Insert the stamen into the center of the flower petal and tape the bottom wires together. Mount with tape, each flower to the top of a taped 14- or 16-gauge stem wire, cut to the desired length. Curve the petal right side in and flare back at the top.

Leaves

Make 3 or 4, in green. The leaves shown in Color Plate 2 are the Hosta leaves (see Index). They have been added to the Calla Lily arrangement separately, and are not attached to the flower stems.

3¼″ in diameter.
See also color plate 18.

CARNATION (*Dianthus Caryophyllus*)

This lacy carnation is a large one, but soft in its effect in a large arrangement, and it can be used as a focal point surrounded by smaller flowers, or in combination with other large ones as shown in the yellow and white arrangement in Color Plate 18.

Materials

Beads: 2 bunches beads for flower and bud; 1½ bunches green for leaves and calyx

*Wires: one 14-gauge for stem or three 16-gauge for flower; one
16-gauge for bud; 26-gauge spool for all parts*

Flower Petals

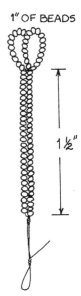

1" OF BEADS

1½"

Fig. 38

Unit 1. Make 27—5 for the bud, and 22 for the flower. Crimp the
open end of the beaded spool wire and push 1½" of beads to the
crimped end of the wire. Four inches from the crimped end of the
wire, make 3 continuous beaded loops, measuring 1" of beads for
each loop. Push 1½" of beads to the base of loop 3, and push the
original 1½" of beads to the base of loop 1. Twist the bare wires
together at the opposite end of the double row of 1½" of beads and
cut away the crimped end. Fig. 38.

Unit 2. Make 6. Crimp the open end of the beaded spool wire.
Five inches from the crimped end, make 11 continuous loops, measuring 1" of beads for each loop. Keep the loops straight across the
bottom and ⅛th of an inch apart at the base. Fig. 39. Bring both
end wires together under the middle loop (the 6th), and 1/3rd of
an inch below it. Twist both wires together for ¼".

Bring beaded wire up to the base of loop 6 to create the first beaded
row. Pass between the bottom of loops 5 and 6 with bare wire,
cross to the left of loop 6, and forward between loops 6 and 7
with bare wire, then bead down to the bottom of the 1st beaded row,
thus making the 2nd row of beads. Create a 1 bead point and
wrap bare wire around the bottom bare wire at the base of the 2
rows of beads. Bead up the right side of the 1st row of beads, thus
creating a 3rd row of beads. Pass to the back between the bottom
of loops 6 and 5, with bare wire, cross bare wire to the right of
loop 5, and forward between loops 5 and 4 with bare wire. Bring
beaded wire down the right side and to the bottom of the 3rd row
of beads, thus creating a 4th row of beads. Wrap bare spool wire
around the wire at the base of the 4 rows of beads, creating a 1-bead
point. Bring beaded wire up the left side of the 4 rows of beads,
thus creating a 5th row of beads. Pass to the back, and between the
bottom of loops 7 and 8, with bare wire, cross to the left of the 8th
loop and forward between loops 8 and 9. Bring beaded wire down
the left side of the 5th row of beads, thus making the 6th row of
beads. Create a 1-bead point and wrap bare spool wire around the
bottom wire. Bead up the right side of the 6 rows of beads, thus
creating the 7th row of beads. Pass to the back between loops 5 and
4 with bare wire, to the right of loop 4 and forward between loops

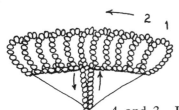

Fig. 39

4 and 3. Bring beaded wire down the right side of the 7 rows of beads, create a 1-bead point, and wrap bare wire around the bottom wire. Bead up the left side of the 8th row of beads, thus creating the 9th row of beads. Pass to the back between loops 8 and 9, to the left of the 9th loop and forward between loops 9 and 10 with bare wire. Bring beaded wire down the left side of the 9 rows of beads, thus creating the 10th row of beads. Create a 1-bead point and wrap spool wire around the bottom wire. Bring beaded wire up the right side of the 10 rows of beads, thus creating the 11th row of beads. Pass to the back and between loops 3 and 2, cross to the right of loop 2, and forward between loops 2 and 1 with bare wire, then bring beaded wire down the right side of the 11th row of beads, thus creating the 12th row of beads. Make a 1-bead point and wrap spool wire around the bottom wire. Bead up the left side of the 12 rows of beads, pass to the back between loops 9 and 10, forward between loops 10 and 11, thus creating the 13th row of beads. Bring beaded wire down the left side of the 13 rows of beads, thus creating the 14th row of beads. Make a 1-bead point, twist both wires together for the length of the original bottom wire, and cut the wire from the spool. Fig. 40.

Flower Calyx

Make 9 continuous 3-row crossover loops, measuring 3″ of beads for the initial loop. Skip lace ⅓ of the way up from the bottom. Fig. 16. Close the calyx by folding it in half, wrong side in, and twisting the lacing wires together for ½″. Cut away all but ¼″ of the lacing wires, and tuck them in. Let the bottom wires hang free. Make 1 for each flower, in green.

Bud Calyx

Make 7 continuous 3-row crossover loops, measuring 2½″ of beads for the initial loop. Lace and close the same way as for the flower calyx. Make 1 for each bud, in green.

Leaves

BASIC: 2½″, pointed top, round bottom, 7 rows.

Cut open the basic loop at the bottom of the loop. Allow 2″

48

Fig. 40

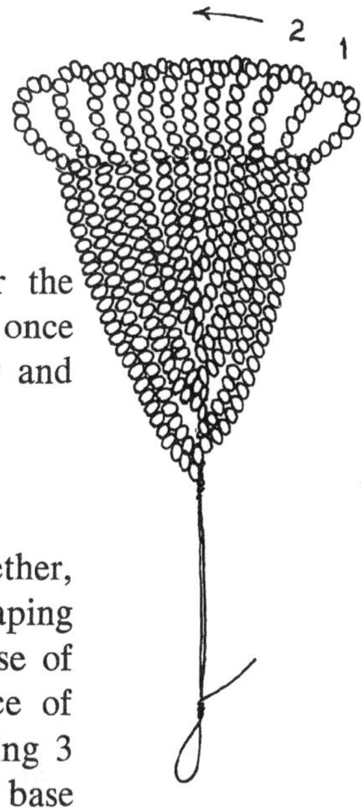

of bare spool wire and cut the wire from the spool. Cover the combined bottom wires with tape. Lace each leaf individually once through the middle, right sides up. Make 10 (6 for the flower and 4 for the bud), in green.

Assembly of Flower

Cut and tape a 14-gauge wire (or 3 16-gauge wires taped together, side by side). Combine the bottom wires of 5 Unit 1's by taping them together. With tape, attach the stem wire close to the base of the beading of the combined 5 Unit 1's. Attach a long piece of 30- or 32-gauge lacing wire to the base of the 5 units, wrapping 3 or 4 times, tightly. Add the remaining 17 of Unit 1 around the base of the first 5, wrapping the wire twice, tightly, with each addition. Add the 6 petals of Unit 2 in the same way, around the base of the 22 of Unit 1. When all of the units have been added, thin out the wires no longer than 2", and cover the wires with tape. Insert the opposite end of the flower stem into the center of the flower calyx. Push the flower calyx up close to the base of the flower, and tape the wires to secure the calyx.

Three inches from the base of the flower, tape on a pair of leaves, directly opposite one another, right sides up. Tape down the stem for 2" and add a second pair of leaves. Tape down the stem another 2" and tape on the 3rd pair of leaves, then tape to the bottom of the stem.

Assembly of Bud

Tape a piece of 16-gauge stem wire 10" in length. To the top of the stem wire, tape on the remaining 5 petals of Unit 1. Insert the opposite end of the stem wire into the center of the bud calyx. Push the calyx up to the base of the bud and tape the calyx wires to the stem wire.

Two inches below the base of the bud, tape on a pair of leaves, directly opposite each other, right sides up. Two inches below the first pair, tape on a second pair in the same way, and tape to the bottom of the stem. Tape the bud stem to the flower stem 1" below the lowest pair of leaves. Bend the flower head and the bud head forward and curl the leaves as shown in the photograph.

3½" x 3¼". See also color plate 19.

CASTOR BEAN LEAVES (*Ricinus communis*)

The castor-oil plant is a native of Africa and its striking foliage is handsome, not only because of its unusual 9-fingered pattern, but because of the various colorings which change during its growth. The young leaves are a deep garnet, changing from green to brown to beige as they mature and increase in size.

Materials for one

Beads: 4½ strands for each group of 9 leaves
Wire: 26- or 28-gauge spool
Tape: Brown or twig
All leaves have pointed tops and round bottoms
Unit 1. BASIC: 10 beads, 5 rows. Make 2 for each leaf.
Unit 2. BASIC: 10 beads, 7 rows. Make 2 for each leaf.
Unit 3. BASIC: 15 beads, 7 rows. Make 2 for each leaf.
Unit 4. BASIC: 15 beads, 9 rows. Make 3 for each leaf.
Reduce all bottom wires to 2. Trim off the top basic wires to ¼" and turn down the wrong side. Cover the bottom wires with ½-width brown or twig tape.

Assembly of Leaf

Part 1. Stack the individual leaves in the following order: one unit 1 on top of one unit 2, these 2 on top of one unit 3, these 3 on top of one unit 4. Have the bottoms even, twist the bottom wires together 2 or 3 times to hold them, and form them into a half circle.
Part 2. Stack the same as for Part 1, but place 2 unit 4's on the bottom, thus using the 3rd unit 4. Twist the bottom wires together and form into a half circle. For Part 1, swing the top leaves to the right, and for Part 2, swing the top leaves to the left. Fig. 41.

Combine the two parts by having each corresponding size opposite each other; unit 1 opposite unit 1, unit 2 opposite unit 2, etc., and

50

tape the combined wires to a short piece of taped 16- or 18-gauge stem wire to reinforce.

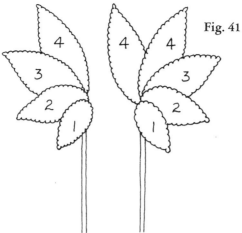

Fig. 41

Flower, 1½" in diameter. See also color plate 5.

CHRYSANTHEMUM—*Button Type*

Smaller than the cushion chrysanthemums, these button "mums" are simple to construct, and make an excellent filler for all types of arrangements.

Materials for one

Beads: 5 strands for flower; 5 strands for leaves
Wires: 26- or 28-gauge spool; 16-gauge for stems

Flower

Allow 3" of bare wire at both ends of each unit.

Unit 1. Make 7 continuous 4-row crossover loops, measuring 1″ of beads for the initial loop. Make 1.

Unit 2. Make 7 continuous 4-row crossover loops, measuring 2¼″ of beads for the initial loop. Make 1.

Unit 3. Make 10 continuous 4-row crossover loops, measuring 2¾″ of beads for the initial loop. Make 1.

Assembly

Follow the Cushion Mum directions for the pattern for leaves and the assembly.

Flower, 5¼″ in diameter.
See also color plate 19.

CHRYSANTHEMUM (*Football "mum"*)

The extra large chrysanthemum, shown in Color Plate 19 with the peacock feathers, is almost twice as large as the ordinary variety. It is particularly attractive when it is made in two colors because the petals appear to be two-shaded. Butterscotch and brown, pumpkin and bittersweet, light and dark red, lavender and purple are all excellent combinations.

Materials for one

Beads: 4 bunches light, 4 bunches dark beads; 1 bunch green
Wires: 26-gauge spool; one 14- or four 16-gauge for stem; two 16-gauge stem for leaves

Flower

There are 8 units to each flower, and all but the first 2 are made with four-row crossover loops. Allow 3″ of bare wire at the beginning and the end of all units.

Unit 1. Make 3 continuous loops measuring 1½″ of beads for each loop. Make 1.

Unit 2. Make 10 continuous loops measuring 2¼″ of beads for each loop. Make 1.

Unit 3. Units 3 through 8 require quite a few loops, and they are easier to manage if the number of loops required are divided into two parts. We will set the pattern in Unit 3, and you can apply the same technique to Units 4, 5, 6, 7 and 8.

Unit 3 calls for 12 continuous four-row crossover loops, measuring 3″ of beads for the initial loop, then beading up the front of the loop, and down the back. (See General Instructions chapter on Cross-overs.) If you work six four-row crossover loops, cut the wire from the spool, repeat it one more time, and join the 2 sections together, you will have accomplished the same thing, and the unit is easier to manipulate. Join the two sections by placing one on top of the other, loops up, wires down, then twisting the pairs of wires together. Unfold the loops into a circle of 12 four-row crossover petals.

Unit 4. 14 continuous four-row crossover loops, measuring 3¾″ of beads for the initial loop before the crossover. Divide the unit into two sections of 7 crossover loops each, and join them. Make 1.

Unit 5. 16 continuous four-row crossover loops, measuring 4½″ of beads for the initial loop before the crossover. Divide it and make 2 sections of 8 four-row crossover loops, and join them. Make Units 1, 2, 3, 4 and 5 all in one color. It can be either the lighter or the darker color, as long as the units are the same.

Unit 6. 20 continuous four-row crossover loops, measuring 5¼″ of beads for each initial loop before the crossover. Divide it and make 2 sections of 10 crossover loops each, and join them. Make 2, one in the light color, and one in the dark.

Unit 7. 20 continuous four-row crossover loops, measuring 5½″ of beads for the initial loop. Divide, and make 2 sections of 10 each and join them. Make one Unit 7 in the lighter shade and one in the darker.

Unit 8. 22 continuous loops (four-row crossover), measuring 6″ of beads for the initial loop. Divide it, make 2 sections of 11 loops each and join them. Make 1 in the lighter shade and 1 in the darker.

Flower Calyx in green

BASIC: 12 beads, round top, round bottom, 12 rows. Make 1 for each flower.

After executing the second row, insert a round pencil in between the 2 rows of beads to shape them into a circle. Fig. 42. Continue wrapping beads around the circle until you have completed 12 rows in all. Because the pattern calls for an even number of rows, you will finish at the top, where the single wire is. Cut the wire from the spool, leaving only 2″, cut open the basic loop at the bottom of the loop and twist both pairs of wires together. Bring both pair through the open circle in the middle, from the wrong side to the right side of the calyx. Make 1 for each flower.

Assembly of Flower

Place Unit 1 into the center of Unit 2, and twist both sets of wires together tightly. Insert the combined Units 1 and 2 into the center of Unit 3 and twist the wires together. Insert the combined Units of 1, 2, and 3 into the center of Unit 4, and twist the wires. Continue in this manner until all but the 2nd Unit 8 has been added. This unit should be laced. It will make the entire flower firmer.

To lace the second Unit 8, cut a 12″ piece of lacing wire (30- or 32-gauge) and thread it into a large darning needle. With a running stitch, go under 2 rows at a time, 1″ up from the bottom of the loops. Sew all the way around the unit. When the sewing is finished, remove the needle, and pull the lacing wires together, cut off all but ½″ and tuck the ½″ of twisted wire inside the unit. Insert the combined units of the flower into the center of the second Unit 8 and twist all wires together. Cup all of the loops of Units 1, 2, 3, 4, 5, and 6 toward the center of the flower to form a semi-ball. Curl the loops of the remaining units out and back.

This is a very heavy flower and will need a strong stem wire to support it. Use either 1 14-gauge or 4 16-gauge wires taped individually, then taped together, side by side. Cut the 16-gauge wires to the desired length before combining them. Insert one end of the stem wire into the base of the flower as far as it will go. Tape on, very securely. Insert the other end of the stem wire into the center of the calyx. Push the calyx up to the base of the flower as far as it will go, and tape the calyx wires to the flower stem.

If you wish to use this flower in an arrangement with other flowers, it will need leaves. Follow the pattern for the Spoon Mum leaves. Make 6 for each flower.

Cut two pieces of 16-gauge stem wires 9″ long for the leaves, and tape them. To the top of each wire, tape a leaf. Show 1″ of stem

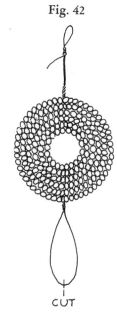

Fig. 42

CUT

on each leaf. Tape down the stem for 1½″ and tape on another leaf on the left side of the stem. Tape down another 1½″ and tape on a 3rd leaf on the right side of the stem. Make 2 sprays of 3 leaves each.

Six inches from the base of the flower, on the left side of the flower stem, tape on one spray of leaves. Tape down the stem for another 2″ and add the 2nd spray of leaves on the right side of the flower stem.

24″ x 8¼″. See also color plate 21.

CONSOLE LAMPS

The console lamps can be used as wall sconces, electrified or not, and there is no end to the possibilities regarding shape and size. The ones shown here, and the smaller boudoir lamps in Color Plate 21 both use the same flower as decorations, plus extra petals all around the frame. Both pairs are made with ¼″ satin bugle beads, but regular 11° beads are just as effective.

The frames of the lamps are shaped by hand and are made in 2 sections, then combined with masking tape. The large pair used 4 pieces of taped 14-gauge wire (2 pieces for each frame), 35″ long and shaped as in Fig. 43, then taped together as indicated. A wire hanger can be straightened and rebent also.

Fig. 43

Materials for one lamp

Beads: 10 bunches
Wire: 26- or 28-gauge spool

Frame Petals

There are 52 petals around the edge of each large frame, spaced about ½″ apart.

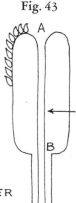

A

B

TAPE
TOGETHER

BASIC: ½", pointed tops, round bottoms, 9 rows.

For each large lamp, there are 3 groups of 9 petals, each mounted on three 16-gauge wires at the top for a crown, and this is repeated for the bottom of the frame. These are also spaced ½" apart, and all petal wires are taped before mounting.

Flowers

There are 15 flowers for each lamp, and each flower has 10 petals, the same size as all of the others. Work the petals of the flowers with a generous basic loop, about 12" (6" when folded).

Flower Centers

Unit 1. Make 1 for each flower, in same color as petals. Make 10 continuous loops, measuring 1" of beads for each loop, and use a large bead of a contrast color to cover the bottom of the loops. A small gold button is attractive. When the 10 loops are finished, back-weave the spool wire halfway around to balance the wires. Allow 3" of bare spool wire, and cut it from the spool. Place the large center bead onto the 3" of wire, cross the wire to the opposite side of the loops, and twist both wires together on the underside of the loops to form a stem.

Unit 2. Make 1 for each flower. There are 9 large teardrop beads, and each one is wrapped around with a row of the same beads with which the petals were made. The teardrops are available with either a metal shank (loop) or a hole at the bottom, and either style may be used.

Cut a piece of spool wire about 30" long. Three inches from one end place a teardrop, and twist the wire twice to secure the teardrop. From the opposite end, feed on enough small beads to wrap around the outer edge of the teardrop, and twist the spool wire twice, to secure. Feed on 3 beads, if you are using the bugle beads, 4 beads if you are using the regular 11° beads, then 1 teardrop. Twist the wires at the base of the teardrop to secure, then feed on enough small beads to wrap around the outside edge of the 2nd teardrop. Continue in this manner until you have wrapped around 9 teardrops, each one separated by 3 beads, if they are bugles, (4 beads if they are 11°). Fig. 44. Back weave the end wire half way around to balance the wires (same as for Unit 1).

Fig. 44

Assembly of Flowers

Insert 1 unit 1 in the center of 1 unit 2, and combine both sets of wires in the center of the underside, by twisting them together to form a stem. Stack 10 petals so that the bottoms are even, and twist all wires together to form the flower stem. Shape the petals into a circle by swinging the top petals to the left, and the bottom petals to the right. Slide the combined center units between two petals, and cover the combined wires with tape. Choose the color tape that best matches the color of the beads. Half-inch masking tape can be used in place of the flower tape, if desired. The masking tape doesn't stretch, but it is firmer.

Tape single petals around the outside edge of the frame ½″ apart, no stem showing.

Build the 6 branches of 9 petals each on the 16-gauge wires, and make 2 groupings of 3 branches each. Fig. 43. Tape on one grouping of 3 branches to the top of the frame (*A*) and tape the other grouping at the bottom of the frame (*B*). Tape all of the flowers to the center double wire, adjusting them so that they fill in the center of the frame, and they are ready to be electrified and mounted either on a wall or permanently anchored into urns, candlesticks, or any other base of your choice.

2-1/3″ in diameter.
See also color plate 5.

CUSHION CHRYSANTHEMUMS

Not all chrysanthemums are huge, and these cushion types and the buttons or pompons as well are a superb addition to an autumn arrangement. Florists use them profusely as fillers as they grow in such a variety of colors.

Materials for one

Beads: 10 strands in a color; 10 strands green
Wires: 26- or 28-gauge spool; 16-gauge for stem

Flower

Allow 3″ of bare wire at both ends of all units.

Unit 1. Make 5 continuous loops measuring 1″ of beads for each loop. Make 1.

Unit 2. Make 7 continuous four-row crossover loops, measuring 2½″ of beads for the initial loop before the crossover. Make 1.

Unit 3. Make 10 continuous 4-row crossover loops, measuring 3″ of beads for the initial loop before the crossover. Make 1.

Unit 4. Make 12 continuous four-row crossover loops, measuring 4″ of beads for each initial loop before crossover. Make 1.

Calyx

Basic: 9 beads, round top, round bottom, 10 rows. Make 1, in green.

Create a basic with 9 beads. Work the second row of beads and wrap bare spool wire twice, at the top of the basic row of beads. Insert a pencil between the 2 rows of beads to make a circle, then continue around the circle of beads until 10 rows have been completed. Cut open the basic loop at the bottom of the loop. Fig. 42. Allow 3″ of bare spool wire and cut the wire from the spool. Bring both pairs of wires through the open circle, from the wrong side to the right side of the calyx.

Leaf

Follow the pattern for the leaf on the Spoon Mum, and mount three of them to a taped piece of 16- or 18-gauge wire. Tape them to the stem of the cushion mum 3″ below the base of the flower. Make 3, in green.

Assembly of Flower

Balance the wires on Units 2, 3, and 4. Twist together the wires of Unit 1, and insert them into the center of Unit 2. Twist both sets of wires together for 1″. Insert the combined Units 1 and 2 into the center of Unit 3, and twist the wires together for 1″. Insert the wires of Units 1, 2 and 3 into the center of Unit 4 and twist all wires together. Tape a piece of 16-gauge wire and add the flower to the top of it with tape. Insert the opposite end of the stem wire into the center circle of the green calyx, and then push the calyx up close to the base of the flower. Tape the calyx wires to the flower stem, and add a spray of 3 leaves.

```
        1           2           3           4
|___|___|___|___|___|___|___|___|___|___|___
```

Fig. 45

FINGER LEAVES (Uniform)

These leaves grouped in threes or fives and mounted on 16-gauge wires make an excellent filler for large or medium-sized arrangements. They give a soft lacy effect. The method for making them is the same as for the leaves used on the Tansy (see Index) except that the "fingers" are all one size.

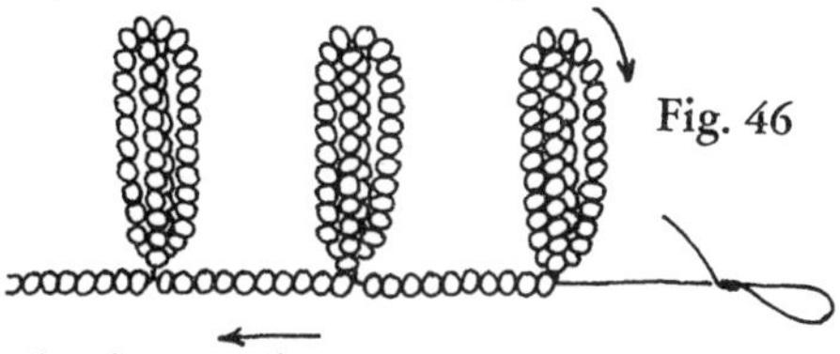

Materials for one leaf

Beads: 2 strands
Wire: 26-gauge spool

Fig. 46

Two inches from the open end of the spool wire, make a narrow loop with 2″ of beads, bead up the front and down the back of the loop, secure the crossover by wrapping bare spool wire around the wire at the base of the loop, thus completing 1 four-row crossover unit. Push 10 beads to the base of the 4-row loop, and at the opposite end of the 10 beads, make another narrow loop of 2″ of beads, then give this second loop a four-row crossover. Fig. 45. Continue until you have made 9 four-row crossover loops, each one separated by 10 beads. Fig. 46. Allow 2″ of bare spool wire and cut the leaf from the spool. Twist together the 2 end wires close to the base of the first and ninth loops. Fig. 47. Give the rows in between the loops one half twist, and shape the loops upward.

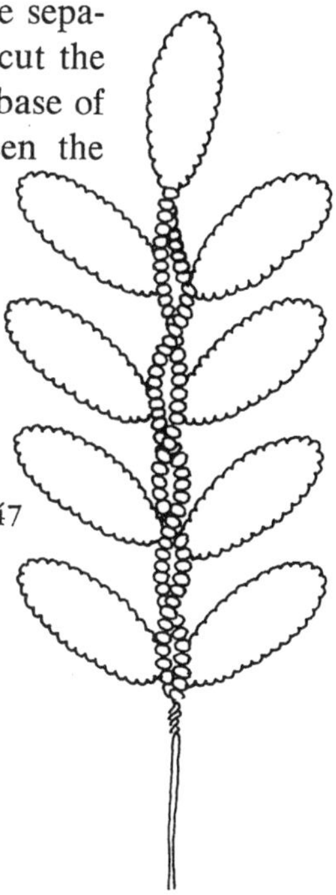

Fig. 47

Stalk, 12″ x 4½″.
Each flower, 2″ x 1¼″.
See also color plate 3.

FOXGLOVE (*Digitalis*)

One of the showiest of all woodland flowers is the foxglove. Its drooping blossoms completely surround a sturdy stalk, and they are tubular in shape, closely resembling the fingers of a glove. The natural color is purple, with a profusion of red or black dots within the tube. However, there are hybrids in white with red dots, and yellow ones with orange dots. The flower is excellent for giving height and width in a 2-sided arrangement. The flowers in white with red dots are shown in Color Plate 3.

Materials for one stalk

Beads: 2½ bunches white; ⅓ bunch for dotting; 2 bunches green for leaves and sepals

Wires: 28-gauge spool for petals and sepals; 26-gauge spool for leaves; 30- or 32-gauge for lacing; 14-gauge for stem (or two 16-gauge)

Flower

Each flower has three small petals and one large one. The large one is dotted. Reverse wrap the spool wire at the top of all petals and reduce the bottom wires to 2. See: General Instruction Chapter; Reducing Wires and Reverse Wrap. Work with a generous basic loop (10″). Make 14 or 16 to a stalk.

Small Petals

BASIC: 12 beads, round top, pointed bottom, 7 rows. Make 3 per flower.

Large Petals, one per flower

BASIC: 15 beads, round top, pointed bottom, 9 rows. Make 1 per flower.

When stringing beads for the large petals, pick up 1 bead of a contrast color for every ½″ of the main color. Starting at the bottom of the basic row of beads on the large petal, lace all 4 petals together so that they are even at the bottom. Let the top of the petals be your guide, and lace with the wrong sides facing up. It is not necessary to lace every row; lace only the basic row, the last 2 rows of the large petal, the first 2 of the second petal, the basic row of the second petal, the last 2 of the second petal, the first 2 of the third, the basic of the third, the last 2 of the third, etc. until all have been joined together. Finish off by going back to the first petal and lacing the first 2 rows with the other end of the lacing wire. Fold petals in half, wrong side in; join the 2 ends of the lacing wires, twisting them together for ½″, then cutting away all but ¼″ of the twisted wires. Tuck the short twisted wires to the inside of the flower, and press it flat against the inside of the petals. Twist the bottom wires together to form a stem. Bow out the petals to form a tube, and bend the tops of the petals outward, slightly.

Sepals

BASIC: 3 beads, pointed tops, round bottoms, 5 rows. If they are made individually, reduce bottom wires to 2.
The sepals can be made in two ways, either individually, or in pairs using the single split basic method. See General Instructions chapter for split basic. There will be fewer wires if the split basic is used. Make 4 per flower, in green.

Small Leaves

(For top of stalk.) Make 8 extra pair of green sepals, or 16 single ones, and combine them in pairs; tape the stems.

Large Leaves

BASIC: 5 beads, pointed tops, round bottoms, 17 rows. Make 5, in green.

Work with a generous basic loop (10″), cut open the bottom of the loop, allow 5″ of bare spool wire, and cut the wire from the spool.

Twist the 3 bottom wires together for 1″ to form a stem and tape the stems.

Assembly of Flower

At the base of each flower, attach a 10″ piece of 30- or 32-gauge lacing wire, and add 4 green sepals (or two pair, depending on which method was used to make them). Tape the stems, and push the sepals up to hug the base of the flowers.

Assembly of Stalk

Tape a 14-gauge wire (or 2 of 16-gauge taped together) that has been cut the desired length (about 15″). Around the top of the wire, tape on 8 pairs of the small leaves, spacing them ¼″ apart down the stem. Allow ½″ of stem on each pair of leaves. Around the stalk, tape on the flowers, one at a time, spacing them ¾″ apart down the stem, and allow 1½″ of stem on each flower. Arch the flower stems downward. When the last flower has been added, tape on the 5 large leaves, around the stem, allowing 1″ of stem on each leaf.

Spray, 9¼″ x 3½″.
See also color plate 3.

FREESIA

The freesia is an extremely popular florist flower. The long-throated bell-like blossoms grow in a wide choice of pastel colors. They are South African in origin and are of the iris family, even though they show no resemblance in their contour. The spray of flowers shown consists of 1 bud with 2 petals, 1 bud with 3 petals, and 3 flowers with 5 petals and 3 leaves each.

Materials

Beads: 7 strands of color for buds and flowers; 1 strand in a contrast

color (*usually yellow*) *for stamens; 7 strands green for leaves and calyx.*
Wires: 28-gauge spool for flowers and stamens; 26-gauge spool for leaves and calyx; 16- or 18-gauge for stem

Petals

Start with a basic of 12 beads and allow 9 beads to fall into the basic loop. This petal is worked using the principle of "a single split basic". (See General Instructions chapter, single split.) Use at least 10″ of bare wire in the basic loop. Wrap once around the 12-bead basic, giving the top unit 3 rows in all. Wrap spool wire twice, tightly, at the completion of the 3rd row of beads, and cut away the spool wire close to the base of the beads. Fig. 48. Push the 9 beads to one side of the basic loop, cut open the basic loop at the base of the petal and crimp the open end of the wire to prevent losing the 9 beads. Attach beaded spool wire to the bottom of the 9th bead, twisting the 2 wires together tightly. Encircle the entire unit with beaded wire, wrapping once at the top basic wire, and twice at the bottom wires. Allow 3″ of bare spool wire, and cut the wire from the spool. Trim off the top basic wire as usual. Make 20 for one spray.

Stamen

One inch from the open end of the beaded spool wire, make an 8-bead loop. Push 1″ of beads close to the 8-bead loop. Allow 3″ of bare spool wire, and cut the wire from the spool. Make 2 more in the same way. Combine the 3 units by twisting the 3 wires together, tightly, at the base of the beaded stems. Fig. 49. Make 3 for each flower, in a contrast color.

Calyx

Make 4 continuous loops, measuring 1″ of beads for each loop. (See General Instructions chapter, Continuous Loops.) Make 1 for each flower and 1 for each bud, in green.

Leaves

Basic: 2½″, pointed tops, round bottoms, 5 rows.
    Tape the bottom wires together after cutting open the basic loop at the bottom of the loop, giving each leaf 3 bottom wires for a stem. Make 3 for each spray, in green.

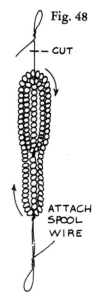

Fig. 48

— CUT

ATTACH SPOOL WIRE

Fig. 49

Assembly of Flowers and Buds

For each flower, lace together 5 petals through the center, at the base of the top unit which has 5 rows, fig. 49a, with the right sides of the petals facing up. Fold the 5 petals in half, wrong sides in, and join the lacing wires by twisting them together for ½". Cut away all but ¼" of the twisted wire and tuck it into the flower, pressing it flat, horizontally, so that it will blend in with the lacing wire. Bow out the top 5 rows to form a cup. Insert the stem wires of the stamens into the center of the flowers, then combine all bottom wires and twist them to form a stem. At the base of each flower, add a calyx, and cover the combined wires with tape.

Assembly of Buds

For the 3-petal buds, lace 3 petals together, close and add a calyx. Tape the combined stem wires. For the 2-petal bud, lace 2 petals together, close, add a calyx, and tape the stems.

Assembly of Spray

To the top of a 10- or 12-inch piece of taped 16- or 18-gauge stem wire, tape the 2-petal bud. One inch below, tape on a 3-petal bud. Add the 3 flowers, spacing them 1" apart, and allow ½" of stem on each bud and flower. One inch below the last flower, tape on the 3 leaves, ½" apart, then continue taping to the bottom of the stem wire.

Fig. 49*a*

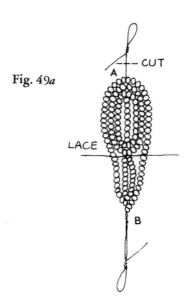

3″ high, 3½″ wide at bottom.

FRENCH LAMP SHADES

Six of these small French shades grace the chandelier in the foyer of my house. The untrimmed shades measure 3″ high, 2½″ across the top, and 3″ across the bottom. They fit over flamelight bulbs.

The frames were purchased untrimmed and decorated with faceted crystal beads strung on 32-gauge wire. The beaded wire was then wrapped continuously, round and round the 4 sections of the frame. The 4 side ribs of the frame were trimmed with beaded wires that had been braided. The bottom ring of the frame has been trimmed with 12 crystal flowers using the largest unit of the primrose. The centers of the flowers are a series of five 12-bead loops worked in real gold beads. To attach the flowers around the bottom rim wrap their wires around the frame securely, several times, then cut away the excess wires close to the base of the flowers.

1   2   3   4   5

Flower, 5" wide.
Leaf, 5" long.
See also color plate 17.

GIANT MATILIJA POPPY (*Romneya coulteri*)

Perhaps the most spectacular wild flower on the Pacific Coast, if not in all America, is the Matilija poppy whose flowers are nearly 6" wide. It is often called the California tree poppy, and its natural colors are smoky yellow, soft orange, and, of course, red.

Materials

Beads: 2 bunches of color for petals; 1 bunch green for leaves and calyx; ½ bunch black for centers
Wires: 26-gauge spool; 16-gauge for bud stem; one 14-gauge or two 16-gauge for flower stem

Flower Petals

The flower petals are very large, measuring 3½" across. Have at least 5 strands of beads on the wire before beginning a petal. The method is "horizontal" basic, the same one that is used for sweet peas, lip petal on lady slipper, etc.

Create a basic loop with bare wire. Fig. 50. Use at least 10" of bare wire in the basic loop (5" when folded in half). Using 14 beads, form a narrow, horizontal loop on the left side of the basic wire, wrap spool wire around top basic wire to secure, then form another narrow 14-bead loop on the opposite side of the basic loop. Fig. 51. Be sure to keep the 2 loops narrow. Wrap spool wire around the bottom basic wire to secure the 2nd 14-bead loop. Circle the outside rim of the 2 horizontal loops, wrapping bare spool wire top and

Fig. 50

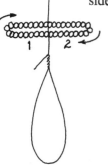

Fig. 51

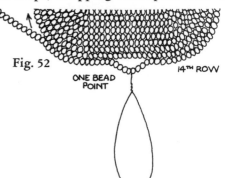

Fig. 52

ONE BEAD POINT

14ᵀᴴ ROW

bottom, Fig. 52, until you have completed 14 rows of beads (7 on each side), round top and round bottom. Starting at the end of the 14th row, create a 1-bead point at the bottom of the petal until 28 rows have been completed (14 on each side). Allow 3″ of bare spool wire and cut the wire from the spool.

Lace each petal, individually, through the middle, working with the right side up. Start the lacing in the middle, and lace to the outside rows. Lock the lacing wire by wrapping it around the lacing wires that join the 2 outside rows of beads, then cut it off, close to the beads. If you find lacing as you work is easier, start the lacing before the 1-bead point, add a row or 2 of beads, lace, add another row or 2 of beads, lace, etc. Make 5.

Fig. 53

Centers

Unit 1. BASIC: 4 beads, round top, round bottom, 12 rows.

Work the first 4 rows round, using a generous basic loop and top basic wire (4″). At the completion of the 4th row, bend the top and bottom wires down. Fig. 73.

For rows 5 and 6 use 12 beads, for rows 7 and 8, use 16 beads, for rows 9 and 10 use 20 beads, and for rows 11 and 12 use 24 beads. This will build a wide beehive. Cut open the basic loop at the bottom of the loop, and join both top and bottom wires in the center of the wrong side of the beehive. Twist the wires together to form a stem and tape them. Make 1, in black.

Unit 2. An inch from the open end of the beaded spool wire make an 8-bead loop. Close the loop with 3 half twists. Have the twists close to the base of the loop, and cut away the 1″ of wire close to the twist. Measure 1½″ of beads and push them close to the base of the 8-bead loop. At the bottom of the 1½″ of beads, make a basic loop, twisting the wires for at least 1″. Measure another 1½″ of beads and top it with a second 8-bead loop. Cut the spool wire close to the base of the second 8-bead loop, and cut open the basic loop at the bottom of the loop, Fig. 53. This constitutes 1 pair. Make 6 pair, in black.

Unit 3. This is made in the same way as Unit 2, except that the measurements are increased. Instead of 1½″ of beads between each 8-bead loop, make it 2″. Make 14 pair, in black.

Flower Calyx

BASIC: 15 beads, round top, round bottom, 18 rows.

1   2   3   4   5

Work the basic and the second row with 15 beads each. At the completion of the 2nd row, wrap bare spool wire twice, tightly, around the top basic wire. Insert a round pencil between the 2 rows of beads and shape the 2 rows into an open circle. Fig. 29. With beaded wire, wrap around the circle, securing bare spool wire at the top and bottom wires until 18 rows have been completed. There will be 9 rows of beads on each side of the circle. Cut open the basic loop at the bottom of the loop. This will give you 2 wires at both ends. Twist both sets of wires together, individually. Fig. 42. Make 1, in green.

Bud Petals

BASIC: 6 beads, round tops, pointed bottoms, 13 rows.

Cup the 3 petals together, wrong sides in, twist together and tape the bottom wires to form a stem. Make 3, in color of petals.

Bud Calyx

BASIC: 10 beads, round top, round bottom, 17 rows.

Join the two leaves together by lacing them, right sides up. Fold them in half, wrong sides in, and close them by twisting the lacing wires together for ½". Cut away all but ¼" of the twisted lacing wires, and tuck the remainder to the inside. Shape the 2 leaves like a funnel, and insert the bud petals. Tape together the bottom wires of both and tape to the top of a taped 16-gauge wire approximately 10" long. Make 2, in green.

Leaves

BASIC: 3", pointed tops, 5 rows plus 4 loopbacks on each side, 8 in all.

Work the basic of 3" and 5 rows, using a long basic loop (12"). Measure 7" of beads for each loopback, creating the 1st, 3rd, 5th, and 7th on the left side of the 5 row unit, and the 2nd, 4th, 6th, and 8th loopback on the right side of the center unit of 5 rows, but work them in succession, 1, 2, 3, 4, etc., and create a pointed bottom as you wraparound the bottom basic loop. For all odd numbered loopbacks, secure the loopbacks by crossing the spool wire over the front of the bottom basic loop, then swing it to the back and forward to the right of the loopback you just completed. This will raise the spool wire back to its original position, before the loopback was made. For all even numbered loopbacks, cross the spool wire normally, front to back and front again (once around the bottom wires).

At the completion of the last loopback, leave on the spool wire enough green beads to reach from the bottom of the leaf to the bottom of the basic row of beads (about 1½"), allow 7" of bare spool wire and cut the wire from the spool. Top trim the bottom part of the right side of the leaf by bringing the 1½" of green beads up the front of the leaf. Insert the open end of the wire through to the back, and down the back of the leaf, twisting it in with the bottom wires of the leaf. Cut away all but 1" of the top basic wire, tape it, and add to it a 10" piece of taped 18- or 19-gauge wire. Bring the heavier wire down the wrong side of the leaf, and tape it to the bottom wires of the leaf. Lace the leaf in 3 places, right side facing up, and include the heavier bracing wire in the lacing. Lock in the lacing wires and trim them off close to the beads. Fig. 54. Make 3 for each flower, in green.

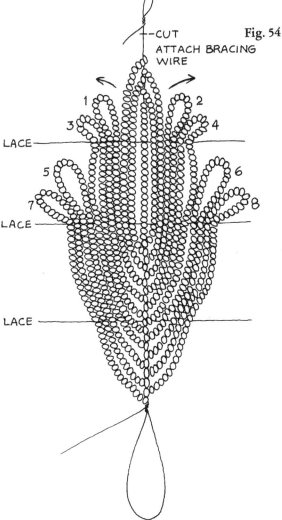

CUT

Fig. 54

ATTACH BRACING WIRE

1 2

3 4

LACE

5 6

7 8

LACE

LACE

Assembly of Flower

Mount, with tape, Unit 1 to the top of a taped 14-gauge stem wire, and attach one end of a 30″ piece of assembly wire. Group the pairs of Unit 2, two pair together. Do the same with the pairs of Unit 3, and add them, one at a time, with the assembly wire, around the base of the mounted beehive, adding the smaller Unit 2's first, then the larger ones. Wrap twice, tightly, with each addition. Cup the petals like a spoon, and add them, one at a time, right sides up in the same manner. When the 5th petal has been added, wrap the assembly wire several times for security, and cut away the excess. Thin out the petal and stamen wires to odd lengths, and cover them with tape.

Turn the calyx wrong side facing up, bring both sets of double wires through the open circle of the calyx and out the right side of the calyx. Insert the open end of the flower stem into the wrong side of the calyx and push the calyx up to the base of the flower. Tape the calyx wires to the stem wire to hold it in place.

Six inches below the base of the flower, tape on the bud stem and 3 leaves. Leave 3½″ of stem on the bud and none on the leaves.

4″ x 1¼″. See also color plate 18.

GIANT TRITOMA (*Kniphofia*)

One of the most startling of autumn-blooming flowers, with dense spikes in vibrant shades of yellows, reds, and oranges that tower regally over everything else like 4th of July skyrockets, the tritoma is also known as Red Hot Poker, Torch lily and Flame flower. The pattern here calls for white and several shades of yellow.

Materials for one

Beads: 1½ strands white; 1¼ strands pale yellow; 3 strands bright

yellow; 4½ strands deep yellow or mustard
Wires: 26- or 28-gauge spool; 14- or 16-gauge for stem

Flower

All of the units for the tritoma are made with continuous loops. Allow 2″ of bare spool wire at both ends of all units.

Unit 1. Make 6 continuous loops measuring 1¼″ of beads for each loop. Make 2, in white.

Unit 2. Make 8 continuous loops, measuring 1½″ of beads for each loop. Make 2, in pale yellow.

Unit 3. Make 10 continuous loops, measuring 2″ of beads for each loop. Make 3, in bright yellow.

Unit 4. Make 11 continuous loops, measuring 2½″ of beads for each loop. Make 3, in deep yellow.

Assembly

Tape a long stem wire. Use 16-gauge for 12- or 14-inch height, and 14-gauge for more than 14 inches high. To the top of the stem wire, tape one Unit 1, shaping the loops upward and around the top of the stem. Tape the second Unit 1, ½″ lower, arranging the loops so that they encircle the loops of the 1st set of loops. Balance the wires of all the remaining units, and slip them on by inserting the open end of the stem wire in the center of each unit. Push up each newly added unit so that it covers the bottom half of the unit that preceded it. Secure each unit with half-width tape for ½″ and cut away any unit wires that extend below the taping. This will keep the stem thin, and allow each newly added unit to slide smoothly up the stem. Shape all loops upward, and when the last unit has been added, tape to the bottom of the stem.

| 1 | 2 | 3 | 4 | 5 |

4″ in diameter.
See also color plate 18.

GINNY ROSE

The Ginny Rose is not a true adaptation of any particular flower; rather it encompasses the best parts of several. Color combinations are optional and it is quite spectacular in any shade. A large flower, it can be used most successfully as a focal point of interest in any large bouquet (Color Plate 18), or alone in a low container.

Materials

Beads: 8 strands for 40 florets; 1 strand of contrast color for centers (usually yellow); 7 strands of contrast color for throat; 3 strands pale green for floret calyx; 1 bunch medium green for leaves and flower calyx
Wires: 26- or 28-gauge spool; one 14- or two 16-gauge for stem; 30- or 32-gauge lacing

Florets

Create a 6-bead loop 4″ from the open end of the spool wire, and wrap the outer rim of the 6-bead loop with a row of beads. Close to the base of the first wrapped loop, make another 6-bead loop, and wrap around it with a row of beads. Continue until there are 4 double loops in all. Fig. 10. Allow 4″ of bare spool wire and cut the wire from the spool. Cross the 4″ of the finish wire under petal 1, up between petals 1 and 2, put on 4 beads in a contrast color, and cross the wire over the center of the flower and down between petals 3 and 4. Twist the 2 wires together for 1″ in the center of the underside of the floret to form a stem, and cover the wires with half-width green tape. Make 40.

Calyx for Florets

Make 5 continuous loops of beads, measuring 1″ of beads for each loop. Make 10, one for every 4 florets, in pale green.

Assembly of Florets and Calyx

Using ½-width tape, combine the stems of 4 florets 1½″ below the base of the flowers. At the same place, attach one calyx. Make 10 groupings of 4 florets and one calyx.

Throat in contrasting color

Unit 1. Make 12 continuous narrow loops of beads, measuring 2″ of beads for each loop. Leave at least 4″ of bare wire at both ends of the unit. Close the unit by bringing the finish wire under loop 1, drawing loops 1 and 2 close together. Bring the wire up between the 1st and 2nd loop, down between the 2nd and 3rd loops, up between the 3rd and 4th loops and down between the 4th and 5th loops, thus back weaving and balancing the two wires so that they are opposite one another. Bring the 2 wires to the center of the underside of the unit, and twist them together for an inch or so. Make 1.

Unit 2. Make 20 continuous narrow loops of beads, measuring 2¼″ of beads for each loop. Leave at least 4″ of bare wire at both ends. Balance the two wires the same as for Unit 1, but do not twist the wires together. Make 1, in same color as Unit 1.

Unit 3. Make 20 continuous narrow loops of beads, measuring 3″ of beads for each loop. Skip lace the 20 loops together, through the middle. Fold the unit in half, with the wrong side of the lacing to the inside, twist together the lacing wires, cut away all but ¼″ of the lacing wires, and tuck it in between the beaded loops. Twist the bottom wires together, cut an 8″ piece of 26- or 28-gauge wire, hook it between the 9th and 10th loops to form another double wire opposite the other two, twist the two new wires together, and set the unit aside. Make 1, in same color as Units 1 and 2.

Assembly of Flower

Set Unit 1 into Unit 2 and twist the bottom wires together. Set the combined Units 1 and 2 into Unit 3 so that the loops of all 3 units are even across the top. Bring the 2 sets of wires at the bottom of Unit 3 to the combined wires of Units 1 and 2, twist all wires together and cover them with tape. Tape these 3 units to the top of a taped 14-gauge wire, or two 16-gauge wires that have been taped individually and then taped together, side by side. Attach a 30″ piece of lacing wire at the base of the combined units, add 5 groupings of the florets around the base of the center loop units. Wrap tightly with each addition. The tops of the florets should be even with the tops of the loops of the center units. Add the remaining 5 floret groupings, one at a time, between the first 5, and at the same level. When all florets have been added, wrap 3 or 4 times around the stem with the assembly wire and cut away the excess. Cover the exposed wires with tape.

Flower Calyx

BASIC: ¾" round top, pointed bottom, 9 rows. Make 5, in green.

Reduce the bottom wires to 2 by cutting open one side of the basic loop at the base of the leaf, twist bottom wires together and cover with tape. Lace the 5 leaves together, one to the other, right sides up, at the bottom of the basic row of beads. Fig. 55. Fold in half, with the wrong side of the lacing wire on the inside, twist the lacing wires together for ½", cut away all but ¼" of the twisted wires and tuck them into the wrong side of the laced leaves. Flair out tops of joined leaves, but do not twist bottom wires together.

Insert the open end of the flower stem into the top of the circle of calyx leaves, and push the calyx up close to the base of the flower. Cover exposed calyx wires with tape to secure it to the stem.

Leaves

There are two hands of leaves, each one includes 2 small leaves and 3 large ones, in green.

Small. BASIC: ½", round tops, pointed bottoms, 7 rows. Make 4 for 2 hands.

Large. BASIC: ½", round tops, pointed bottoms, 13 rows. Make 6 for 2 hands.

Tape stem wires on all leaves with ½-width tape. Tape together 2 small leaves and 3 large leaves, as shown in Fig. 55a, for 1 hand of leaves. Repeat for the 2nd hand of leaves, then lace every other row in an arch. Trim the center of each hand of leaves by making a narrow loop of 3" of beads and taping its bottom wires to the leaf wires at the base of the bottom pair of large leaves. Give this loop of beads 2 half twists, flatten the loop against the front of the leaves and secure the top of the loop to the base of the top leaf with a short piece of lacing wire, twist the lacing wire for ½", cut away all but ¼", and flatten it against the wrong side of the hand of leaves.

Four inches below the head of the flower, tape on 1 hand of leaves on the left side of the master stem. Three inches below the first hand of leaves, tape the 2nd hand of leaves. If the flower head is to be short-stemmed and used in a low arrangement, mount each hand of leaves on separate 16-gauge stem wires, and insert in the arrangement near the head of the flower.

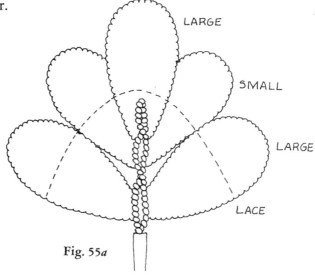

Fig. 55

Fig. 55a

LARGE

SMALL

LARGE

LACE

8½″ x 8½″. See also color plate 6.

GRAPES

There are three clusters of grapes shown in Color Plate 6. Each cluster has 30 grapes, made in French mauve, lavender and celadon green, all transparent.

Materials for one cluster

Beads: 1½ strands for each grape (2½ bunches for 30), 1 bunch green transparent for leaves and grape tip, 30 corks (¾″ diameter)

Wires: 24-gauge coil for grape stems; 16-gauge for mounting leaves and grapes; 28- or 30-gauge spool for grape tips
Water soluble glue and a small paintbrush

Grapes

Each grape has a small green disc at the tip. Make a basic of 3 beads and give it one row of beads on each side (3 rows in all). Keep them round at both ends. Twist together both top basic and bottom basic wires in the center of the wrong side of the green disc. Make one for each grape. Cut 30 pieces of 24-gauge wire (one for each grape) about 9″ long. Bend each wire at one end for ½″ and hook one wire into the base of each green disc. Tape them to secure, wrapping the tape 2 or 3 times for 1″, then taping to the ends of the 24-gauge wires. The extra taping should make a tight fit when the open end of the 24-gauge wire is inserted into the hole of the cork ball. Remove one end of one strand of beads from the bunch of beads, and knot the end of the thread. Remove the opposite end of the strand and knot it also. Insert one knot into the hole of a cork ball, then insert the open end of the disc stem (24-gauge wire) into the hole of the cork. This will secure the thread. Pull the disc stem all the way through so that the green disc rests securely on the top of the cork, covering the hole. Cover half of the cork with glue and wrap threaded beads around and down the cork. Set aside to dry, and work on 8 or 10 more corks in the same way. This will give the glue a chance to set. When it has set, start with the first cork, and add more glue and continue gluing on the remainder of the strand of beads. Start another strand of beads by knotting both ends, and finish covering the rest of the cork with the beads. A square of styrofoam or clay is convenient to use as a holder for the corks as they dry. The trick is to glue only a few rows at a time, let dry for 15 to 20 minutes, then glue a few more rows. Make sure to start the first bead of the second strand of beads close to the last bead of the first strand.

Leaves in green. All have pointed tops and round bottoms

Large. BASIC: 4 beads, 17 rows. Make 3 for each grape cluster.
Medium. BASIC: 4 beads, 13 rows. Make 6 for each grape cluster.
Small. BASIC: 10 beads, 7 rows. Make 6 for each grape cluster.

Cut open the basic loop at the bottom on all leaves, and tape the stems.

Coil

Make a narrow loop with 8″ of beads and coil it around a pen or pencil. Twist the bottom wires and tape them. Make 1 for each set of leaves, in green.

Assembly of Grape Cluster

Tape a 12″ piece of 16-gauge wire. At one end tape on the grapes, one at a time. Vary the lengths of the stems of the grapes. The first 3 or 4 should have 3½″ of stem, the next 4 or 5 should have 3¼″ of stem, etc. Follow this pattern of shortening the stems of the grapes by ¼″ until all 30 grapes have been taped to the 16-gauge wire, working down the stem wire ¼″ as each group of 4 or 5 grapes are added.

Assembly of Leaves

Tape three 12″ pieces of 16-gauge wire, individually, and to the top of each one tape on 1 large leaf, a pair of medium leaves, opposite one another, and one pair of small leaves, opposite one another. Fig. 56. One inch below each small pair of leaves tape on a coiled loop. Combine all 16-gauge stem wires with tape 1″ below the pairs of small leaves. Tape the leaf stems to the grape stems 1″ beyond the last row of grapes. Coil the combined stem wires and fan the leaves across the top of the grapes.

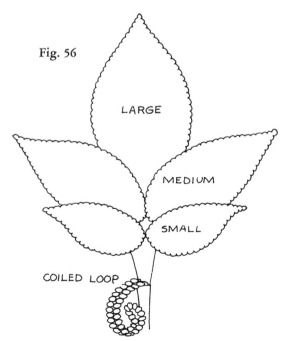

Fig. 56

LARGE

MEDIUM

SMALL

COILED LOOP

Flower, 3¼" in diameter.
See also color plate 8.

HIBISCUS (*Rosa-Sinensis*)

Outstanding among tropical plants is the hibiscus. It grows in great profusion in the Hawaiian Islands, where it is the state flower. The pattern here is for a double yellow hybrid, and the cluster includes 1 flower, a 1-petal bud, a 2-petal bud, and 3 branches of leaves with 3 leaves on each branch.

Materials for one cluster

Beads: 13 strands yellow for petals; 1 bunch green; 3 strands pale green for sepals; 1 strand orange for stamen
Wires: 26- or 28-gauge spool; 30- or 32-gauge spool for assembling; 16-gauge for stem

Flower Petals

Large. BASIC: ½", round tops, pointed bottoms, 13 rows. Make 5, in yellow.
Small. BASIC: ½", round tops, pointed bottoms, 11 rows. Make 4, in yellow.

Flower Stamen

BASIC: ½", round top, pointed bottom, 9 rows. Make 1, in orange.

Bud Petals

BASIC: ½", round tops, pointed bottoms, 13 rows. Reduce to 2 the bottom wires on all petals. Make 4, in yellow.

Sepals

Push 1¼" of the pale green beads to the crimped end of the wire. Four inches from the crimped end, make 2 loops of beads measuring 1" of beads for each loop. Push 1¼" of beads to the base of the second beaded loop, and twist the bottom wires together. Fig. 38.

78

Make 9 (2 for the small bud, 3 for the large bud, and 4 for the flower), all in pale green.

Leaves

BASIC: 1″, pointed top, round bottom, 9 rows.
Leave 3 wires at the base of all leaves by cutting open the basic loop at the bottom of the loop. Twist all three wires together and tape them. Make 9, in green.

Assembly of Flower

Stack the 4 smallest petals, one on top of the other, bottoms even, right sides up, and twist the bottom wires together. Swing the petals into a circle, and lift the petals up and out to form a throat. In between any 2 petals, slide the stamen petal that has been coiled. Wrap the stem wires of the stamen around the wires of the small petals. Attach a 20″ piece of lacing wire to the base of the petals, and add 4 sepals, one at a time, around the base of the petals, wrapping the lacing wire twice, tightly, with each addition. Add the 5 large flower petals in the same way, around the base of the small petals and sepals. Shape the larger petals up and out to conform with the shape of the smaller ones. Wrap lacing wire 3 or 4 times more, for security, cut away the excess, and tape the combined wires.

Assembly of Large Bud

Stack 3 large petals the same as for the 4 small petals of the flower, twist the bottom wires together, cup the 3 petals, wrong sides in, slightly overlapping one another, attach a 12″ piece of lacing wire to the base of the 3 petals, and add 3 sepals around the base of the 3 petals. Cover the bottom wires with tape.

Assembly of Small Bud

Spiral one petal, lengthwise, wrong side in, and attach 2 sepals around the base of the petal with either tape or lacing wire.

Assembly of Leaves

Tape together the stems of 3 leaves, setting the center one ¼″ higher than the other 2. Repeat for 2 more sets of 3 leaves each. Mount each group of 3 leaves to the top of a piece of taped 16-gauge stem wire that has been cut 7 or 8 inches long.

Assembly of Grouping

Mount each flower and each bud to the top of a piece of taped 16-gauge wire, cut to the desired length—6" for the flower, 4 and 5 inches for the buds. Gather together all stem wires so that they are even at the bottom, and tape them together, starting the tape 3" up from the bottom.

This grouping can have beaded stems using the large stem beads if you wish. See General Instructions for Beaded Stems.

7½" x 2⅛". See also color plates 2, 7.

HOSTA LEAVES (*Funkia*)

These large leaves make an excellent filler in any bouquet where side line or background effect is needed. They may be made in solid green or striped in white. If striping is desired, it need not be regular, for example, vary every other row on each side of the basic in green and every other row in white, or pre-string 6 or 7 inches of green, 3 or 4 inches of white, 6 or 7 inches in green, etc. and let the shading fall where it may.

Materials for one leaf

Beads: 7½ strands; 3½" of large stem beads are optional
Wires: 30- or 32-gauge spool for lacing; 26-gauge spool; 18-gauge stem for bracing; 19-gauge stem is optional

If large green stem beads and 19-gauge wires are available, create a basic row with 3½" of stem beads on a 12" piece of 19-gauge stem wire by taping one end of the 19-gauge wire for 3". Onto the opposite untaped end, place the 3½" of stem beads, and cover the remaining part of the 19-gauge stem wire with tape. Fig. 27. Attach the open end of the beaded spool wire to the base of the beads, wrapping the spool wire 3 or 4 times to secure it, then proceed with the making of the leaf until you have completed 23 rows in all, making a pointed top and a round bottom. Lace the leaf in 3 places, once through the middle, halfway down from the top, and halfway up from the bottom. Lock in the ends of the lacing wires and cut away the excess, close to the beads.

If stem beads and 19-gauge wires are not to be used, make the leaf in the usual way, lacing as you work, creating a 3½" basic and 23 rows, pointed top, and round bottom. Reinforce with a 10" piece of taped 18-gauge stem wire by attaching it to the top basic wire, with tape, bringing the 18-gauge wire down the back of the leaf and taping the bottom wires together. Secure the reinforcing wire to the center of the leaf with a small piece of lacing wire, twist the lacing wire for ½", cut away all but ¼" of the twisted lacing wire, and press it flat against the wrong side of the leaf.

Spray, 9½" x 4".
See also color plate 3.

LADY BELL (*Campanula*)

This is a simple flower to make, and in its simplicity lies its charm. Lovely in delicate pinks, blues, lavenders, and yellows, it adds grace and line to either a large or small bouquet.

Materials

Beads: 6 strands of color for flowers; 8 strands green for leaves and calyx; 1 strand in contrast color for stamens
Wires: 26- or 28-gauge spool; 18-gauge for stem

Flower

Unit 1. Make 3 continuous 4-row crossover loops, measuring 2¼" of beads for the initial loop. Make 1 for each flower.

Unit 2. Make 6 continuous 4-row crossover loops, measuring 2¼″ of beads for the initial loop. Make 1 for each flower.

Stamens

Three inches from the open end of the beaded spool wire, make a 7-bead loop. Close the loop with 2 tight twists, cut away 1 wire, close to the base of the loop, and onto the remaining wire transfer 1″ of green beads. Make 3, and combine them by twisting together the wires at the opposite end of the green beads. Fig. 49. Make 3 for each flower, in a contrast color.

Calyx

Make 6 continuous loops measuring 1″ of beads for each loop. Make 1 for each flower, in green.

Leaves

BASIC: 2½″, pointed tops, round bottoms, 5 rows. Tape the bottom wires together. Make 9, in green.

Assembly of Flower

Insert a cluster of 3 stamens into the center of one Unit 1 and twist the bottom wires together for ½″. Insert the combined cluster of stamen and Unit 1 into the center of one Unit 2, twist the bottom wires together, set these units into a calyx, and cover all wires with tape to form a stem. Shape the loops of Units 1 and 2 up and out to form a trumpet effect, and bring the calyx loops up close to the base of the flower.

Assembly of Cluster

Tape 3 pieces of 18-gauge wire. Cut one 9½″ long, one 8″ long and the third one 7″ long. To the top of the 9½″ stem wire, tape 1 flower. Add 1 leaf 3½″ below the base of the flower. To the top of the 8″ stem wire, tape on 1 flower. Add 2 leaves 3″ below the base of the flower. To the top of the remaining 7″ stem wire, tape 1 flower. Add 3 leaves 3½″ below the base of the flower. Stack all stem wires so that they are even at the bottom. Three inches above the bottom, tape on the remaining 3 leaves, and continue taping to the bottom of the stem wires.

4¾'' x 4''. See also color plates 10, 16.

MAIDENHAIR FERN (Shaded)

The laciness of maidenhair fern can be an attribute to any bouquet. The shaded variety is particularly attractive because it adds just the right amount of white to any grouping of flowers.

Materials for one spray

Beads: 1½ strands white; 3½ to 4 strands green
Wires: 26-gauge spool, silver or gold; 16- or 18-gauge for stem

Fig. 57

All loops have 12 beads, and each pair of loops is separated by 5 beads.

Unit 1. One inch from the open end of the beaded spool wire, make one 12-bead loop, twisting the wires very close to the base of the loop. Cut away the 1″ of bare wire very close to the base of the loop. Push 5 beads close to the base of the loop, and at the bottom of the 5 beads, make a pair of 12-bead loops, one on the left and one on the right. Push 5 beads to the base of the pair of loops, and at the bottom of the 5 beads, make another pair of 12-bead loops, one on the left and one on the right. Allow 2″ of bare spool wire and cut the wire from the spool. Fig. 57. Make 1, in white.

Unit 2. Make 2. Transfer 3 or 4 strands of green beads to the spool wire, then 41 white beads. Start this unit the same as Unit 1: one 12-bead loop in white, 5 beads, and a pair of 12-bead loops. This will use up the white beads that were in front of the green ones. Push 5 green beads to the base of the pair of white loops, and make a pair of 12-bead loops in green. Allow 2″ of bare spool wire and cut the wire from the spool. Fig. 58. Each time a unit is completed, feed on the 41 white beads that will be used at the beginning of all units.

Units 3, 4, 5, 6 and 7 are made the same way, with the top 3 loops in white, and the others in green. To each unit add another pair of green loops, separating each pair with 5 beads. Unit 3 has

Fig. 58

3 white loops and 2 pair in green; Unit 4 has 3 white loops and 3 pair in green; Unit 5 has 3 white loops and 4 pair in green; Unit 6 has 3 white loops and 5 pair in green, and Unit 7 has 3 white loops and 6 pair in green. Make 2 of Units 3, 4, 5, 6 and 7.

Assembly of Fern

Using half-width tape, attach 1 Unit 1 to the top of a taped 16- or 18-gauge stem wire. Tape down ¼″ and tape on 2 Unit 2s, one on the left and one on the right. Tape down another ¼″ and add 2 Unit 3s, one on the left and one on the right. Continue adding the remaining units in the same way until all units have been taped on. If larger branches are desired, combine 3 sprays together.

Spray, 12″ x 6″.
See also color plate 5.

MEADOW RUE (*Thalictrum aquilegifolium*)

The meadow rue is a small delicate flower with spidery stamens that burst from the center of the small round petals. It is most effective in branch form, but shorter sprigs can be used in smaller arrangements. Its predominant colors are lavender and purple, but there are varieties in pinks and white. The number of flowers and buds corresponds with the photograph above.

Materials

Beads: 2½ bunches lavender for flowers; 8 strands yellow for stamens; 1½ strands green for leaves
Wires: 28-gauge spool; three 16-gauge for stem

Petals

The 4 petals of the flower are made with a single split basic wire in order to eliminate as many bottom wires as possible.

Working with a generous basic loop, create a basic of 5 beads, and slip 5 beads into the basic loop before closing it. Make a 7-row petal around the top 5 beads, keeping the petal round at top and bottom. Wrap spool wire twice, tightly, at the base of the 7th row. Push the 5 beads that are in the basic loop to one side of the loop, and cut open the basic loop at the bottom of the loop, causing it to become 2 wires. Fig. 23. Wrap bare spool wire down and around the wire at the base of the second 5 beads. The length of the wrap should be equal to the distance between the basic beads and the 7th row of beads on the first petal. Wrap beads around these 5 until you have 7 rows, thus completing a pair of petals, all on one wire. Allow 4″ of bare spool wire and cut the petals from the spool. Repeat in the same way for another pair of petals to complete the number needed for one flower. To execute the branch as shown, make 26 pairs for 13 flowers.

Buds

Large. These consist of 1 pair of flower petals, made the same way. To shape them, cup the 2 petals, wrong sides in. Make 4 pairs for 4 large buds.

Small. These consist of 1 pair of petals made the same way, but the number of rows of beads are reduced to 5. The basic is the same (5 beads). Make 10 pairs for 10 small buds.

Stamens

The stamens are made in pairs that are continuous, and each measurement of beads has between it a coil of bare wire that has been wrapped around the pointed end of a darning needle or corsage pin. Gold wire can be used for the stamens, if desired, as the coil will be less obvious. Transfer 1 strand of beads to a spool of 28-gauge wire. One inch from the open end of the wire, wrap bare wire 3 times around the pointed end of the needle or pin. Keep the wraps close together. Remove the needle from the coils. Push 1″ of beads close to the coil, and at the base of the 1″ of beads, make a basic loop in the bare wire. Move 1″ of beads down to the basic loop, and at the top of this second 1″ of beads, wrap bare spool wire around the needle 6 times, keeping the wraps close together. Fig. 59. Cut in the middle of the 6 coils. This forms the starting coil for the next pair. Cut away the 1″ of bare wire at the end of the first coil. Continue in the same way until 6 pairs have been made for each flower; make them in yellow.

Assembly of Flower

Cut open the basic loops of the 6 pairs of stamens at the bottom of the loops. Combine the wires of all 6 pairs, and twist them tightly together. Add 2 pairs of petals around the base of the beaded stamens, and cover the wires with tape all the way to the bottom. These wires will form the stems of the flowers, so leave generous amounts as you work (about 3″ on all petals).

Leaves

BASIC: 5 beads, pointed tops, round bottoms, 5 rows. Twist bottom wires together and tape. Make 9, in green.
There is very little greenery on the meadow rue stems, and the leaves are small.

Assembly of Branches (3)

Leave ½″ stems on all leaves, 1″ stems on all buds, and 2″ stems on all flowers.
Center Branch. To the top of a 12- or 14-inch piece of taped 16-gauge stem wire, tape on 1 small bud. One inch lower, add a large bud; one inch lower add a small bud. Work down the stem, and add the following flowers, each one ½″ lower than the preceding one: 2 flowers, 1 small bud, 2 flowers, 1 small bud, 1 leaf, 1 flower, 1 large bud, 2 leaves and 2 flowers. This completes the center branch.
Left Branch. Combine, on a taped 16-gauge wire, in the following order, 2 small buds, 1 large bud, 2 flowers, 2 small buds, 2 flowers, 1 large bud, 1 small bud, and 1 leaf. Space them ½″ apart and leave the same amount of stems on this branch as you did on the center one.
Right Branch. Combine on another taped 16-gauge wire in the following order: 2 small buds, 1 large bud, 1 leaf, 1 flower, 1 leaf, 1 flower, and 1 leaf. Space in the same way.

With tape, add the 2 shorter branches to the center one below the last leaf of flower on each one.

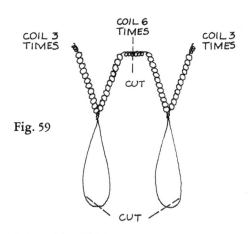

Fig. 59

Spray, 9″ x 5″.
See also color plate 2.

MIMOSA (*Acacia*)

Native to the Southern part of the United States, this profusion of tight yellow blossoms in bell-like clusters is a lovely supplement to any spring bouquet. The grouping shown includes 16 small buds, 15 large buds, 5 small leaves, and 8 large ones.

Materials

Fig. 60

Beads: 1 bunch yellow opaque; ½ bunch green
Wires: 28- or 30-gauge spool for flowers; 28-gauge for leaves; 18-gauge for stem

Flower

Small bud. Three inches from the crimped end of the beaded spool wire, make a narrow loop of 12 beads, and give the loop a 4-row crossover by beading up the front and down the back of the loop. Allow 3″ of bare spool wire, and cut the wire from the spool. Cover the stem with ½-width tape. Make 16, in yellow.

Large bud. Three inches from the crimped end of the beaded spool wire, make 3 continuous 12-bead loops. Keep the loops round. Allow 15″ of bare spool wire and cut the wire from the spool. Bring both wires together at the base of the center loop, and twist them together twice, close to the base of the loop. Insert the open end of the long wire into the center of the first loop and out through the center of the 3rd loop, passing through all 3 loops. Onto the long wire feed on enough yellow beads to cross over the top of the original 3 loops 3 times, thus giving the 3 loops 3 rows of beads over the top. Secure each row of beads by wrapping the long wire once around the single wire at the bottom. In the opposite direction, cross over the top of all loops, once, with a row of beads. Twist both wires together at the bottom of the beaded bud to form a stem, and cover the combined wires with ½-width tape. Make 15, in yellow. Figs. 60, 61, 62.

87

1   2   3   4   5

Assembly of Flower Cluster

Tape 3 pieces of 18-gauge wire with ½-width tape. Cut 1 wire 10″ long and the other two 9″ long. All flowers and leaves are added to the stem wires close to the wire with no stem showing on flowers and leaves. Mount flowers and leaves to the stem wires as shown in Fig. 63, spacing them as directed, then combine all 3 wires with tape.

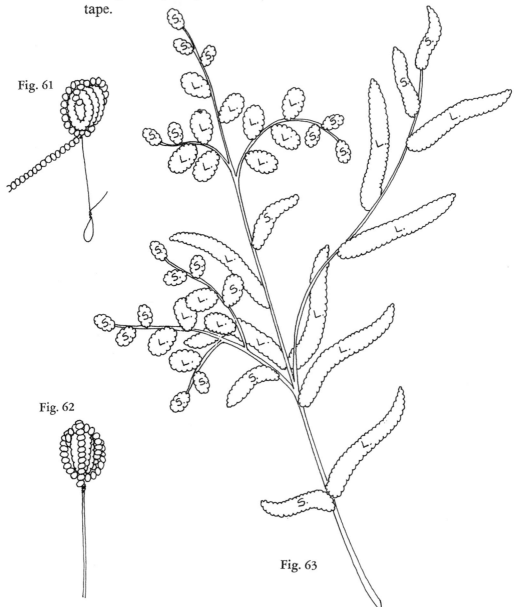

Fig. 61

Fig. 62

Fig. 63

Flower, 3″ in diameter.
See also color plate 17.

MOUNTAIN BLUETS (*Centaurea montana*)

This European perennial is lacy and airy in appearance. It grows in solid white, red or yellow, and also in blue with lavender or pink centers. The pattern is very similar to the one for the cornflower (bachelor button), but there are more petals and they are slightly larger.

Materials for one flower

Beads: 5½ strands for flower; 3 strands green for 2 leaves and 1 calyx

Wires: 26- or 28-gauge spool; 18- or 19-gauge for stems; 30- or 32- gauge for assembling

Flower

Unit 1. Two inches from the open end of the beaded spool wire, make 8 continuous loops, measuring 1″ of beads for each loop. Balance the wires, twist them together, narrow the loops, and give each one a half twist in the middle of the loop. Make 1.

Unit 2. Two inches from the open end of the beaded spool of wire, make 12 continuous loops, measuring 1½″ of beads for each loop. Balance the wires, but do not twist them together. Narrow the loops, and give each one a half twist in the middle. Make 1.

Unit 3. Crimp the open end of the beaded spool wire and push 1″ of beads to the crimped end of the wire. Three inches from the crimped end of the wire, make 3 continuous beaded loops, measuring 1″ of beads for each loop. Push the 1″ of beads to the base of the first loop, measure another 1″ of beads to the first 1″ and wrap bare spool wire around the wire at the base of the first 1″ of beads. Bring beaded spool wire up the left side of the two 1″ rows of beads, force bare spool wire between the base of the 2nd and 3rd beaded loops, bring the wire across the back and to the left of the 3rd loop. Make 2 more 1″ loops of beads to the left of the 3rd loop, bring beaded wire down the left side of the 3 rows of beads and twist the two bottom wires together. Make 8.

1   2   3   4   5

Calyx

Make 7 continuous beaded loops, measuring 1½" of beads for each loop. Make 1, in green.

Assembly of Flower

Insert the twisted wires of Unit 1 into the center of Unit 2, twist both sets of wires together, and tape them. Tape the combined units to the top of a taped piece of 18-gauge wire. At the base of Units 1 and 2, attach one end of a piece of lacing wire by wrapping it tightly 2 or 3 times to secure. Add, one at a time, the 8 petals of Unit 3, wrapping the wire ·twice, tightly, with each addition. Tape down the stem for 1", then cut away all excess petal wires. Add the calyx close to the base of the flower, and tape its wires to the stem wire. Tape on 2 whorl leaves, 3 or 4 inches below the base of the flower. (See index for Whorl leaf.)

If large green stem beads are available, use them on this flower, and follow the instructions for Beaded Stems.

Each leaf, 3" x 2¾".
See also color plate 8.

PALMETTO LEAF

The large lacy leaves shown in Color Plate 8 with the hibiscus and shrimp plant are an embellishment of the leaves used on the cushion, button and Fuji chrysanthemums.

Materials for one leaf

Beads: 3 strands green
Wires: 26-gauge spool; 16-gauge for stem

String 3 strands of green beads on 26-gauge spool wire, and measure 1½" of beads for the basic. Work with a generous basic loop,

1   2   3   4

and make 5 rows, pointed top and round bottom. Make 6 loopbacks on each side of this center unit, measuring 4″ of beads for each loopback. Make the first loopback on the left side of the center unit of 5 rows, crossing the bare spool wire in front, to the back, and forward, to the right of the loopback.

Make the 2nd loopback on the right side of the center unit of 5 rows, and wrap the spool wire once around the bottom basic loop, crossing in front, normally. Make the 3rd loopback to the left of the first loopback, cross the bare spool wire in front, to the back and forward to the right of the third loopback (the one just completed). The direction of the wrap at the completion of the 3rd, 5th, 7th, 9th, and 11th should be the same as for the 1st loopback. The direction of the wrap at the completion of loopbacks 4, 6, 8, 10 and 12 should be the same as for the 2nd. Fig. 64.

At the completion of the 12th loopback, allow 3″ of bare spool wire and cut the wire from the spool. Twist bottom wires together and tape. These leaves can be mounted on taped 16-gauge wires in sprays of 3 or 5 leaves and used as fillers in all types of arrangements.

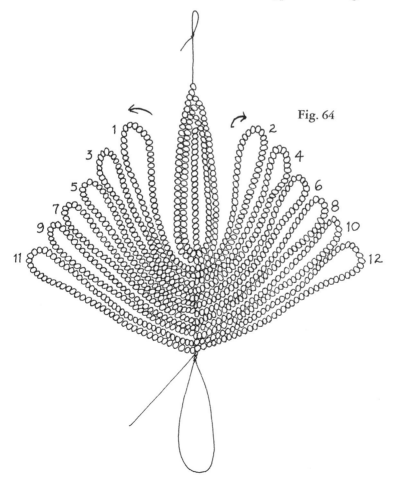

Fig. 64

PEACOCK FEATHERS

The vibrant colors of the peacock feathers were a challenge too great to overlook. Worked on gold wire, the effect is indeed, whimsical. Although the true feathers have delicate feelers the full length of the quill, it is a bit impractical to copy this with the wires as they become entangled with one another so easily. Use them as shown in Color Plate 19 with a football mum, or a dozen or so in a tall vase.

Materials for one feather

Beads: about 4½" each teal blue and pale aqua; about 4" light green; about 17" butterscotch or light topaz
Wires: 26-gauge gold spool; 14- or 16-gauge for stems

String on the spool wire enough teal blue beads to create a basic of 4 beads and 7 rows. Allow approximately 30" of bare spool wire, and cut the wire from the spool. Onto the open end of the 30" bare wire, feed on enough aqua beads to work rows 8, 9, 10, and 11. Feed on enough pale green beads to work the first half of row 12, change to butterscotch beads, and work the top half of row 12 and the top half of row 13 in butterscotch. Feed on enough light green to complete the bottom half of the 13th row and the bottom half of the 14th row. Feed on enough butterscotch beads to make the top half of the 14th row, and the top half of the 15th row. Finish the bottom half of the 15th row with pale green, then feed on enough butterscotch beads to work rows 16, 17, 18, 19, 20 and 21. Allow 3" of bare spool wire and cut away the excess. Cut open the bottom basic loop at the bottom of the loop, reduce the top basic wire to 1½" and tape it. Tape a piece of 14- or 16-gauge stem wire. If the feathers are to be long, use 14-gauge. Tape the stem wire to the top basic wire, and bring the heavy stem wire down the back of the beaded unit (the eye of the feather). Tape the bottom wires of the "eye" to the stem wire. Attach bare spool wire (gold) to the base of the eye, wrapping 3 or 4 times to secure, then form bare wire loopbacks on each side of the eye. Use 8″ of bare wire for each loop-back, working the first one on the left, the second one on the right, etc., until there are 12 loopbacks on both sides of the eye (24 in all). Wrap bare spool wire several times around the base of the last loop-back, to secure, and cut the wire from the spool. Cover the remaining heavy stem wire with either gold silk floss, or gold paint.

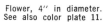
Flower, 4″ in diameter.
See also color plate 11.

PEONY (*Paeonia albiflora*)

There are well over 100 varieties of peonies; this one is probably the most familiar one. Their natural colors run from garnet red to pinks and pure whites, and some have pale yellow centers. A solid color is described here, but the first 2 or 3 center units can be worked in a contrast color if so desired.

Materials

Beads: 1 bunch red for each flower; ½ bunch green
Wires: 14- or 16-gauge for stem; 26-gauge spool

Flower

Unit 1. Make 12 continuous loops, measuring 1″ of beads for each loop. Make 1.

Unit 2. Make 12 continuous loops, measuring 2″ of beads for each loop. Make 1.

Unit 3. Make 15 continuous loops, measuring 2¾″ of beads for each loop. Make 1.

Unit 4. Make 20 continuous loops, measuring 3¼″ of beads for each loop. Make 1.

Unit 5. BASIC: 6 beads, round tops, round bottoms, 21 rows. Make 6. Skip-lace each petal, individually, with the right sides up.

Bud

Make 12 continuous loops, measuring 2″ of beads for each loop. Make 1, in red.

Calyx (Sepals)

BASIC: 5 beads, round tops, round bottoms, 9 rows.
Reduce to 2 the number of wires at the base of all petals and calyx.
Make 9 (4 for bud, and 5 for flower) in green.

Leaves

Large. BASIC: 12 beads, pointed tops, round bottoms, 9 rows. Make 6, in green.
Small. BASIC: 12 beads, pointed tops, round bottoms, 7 rows. Make 4, in green.

Assembly of Flower

Balance the wires of all loop units (1 through 4) by bringing the finish wire at the bottom of the last loop under the first loop to close the loops, then up between loops 1 and 2, down between loops 2 and 3, up between loops 3 and 4, down between loops 4 and 5, etc. until the 2 end wires are opposite one another. Twist together the 2 wires of Unit 1, and insert them into the center of Unit 2. Twist the wires of Units 1 and Unit 2 together, and insert them into the center of Unit 3. Twist the wires of Units 1, 2 and 3 together, and insert them into the center of Unit 4. Twist all wires together and tape them. Insert a taped 16-gauge stem wire into the center of the bottom of the combined units, and securely tape the wires to one another. Cut a 20″ piece of 30- or 32-gauge assembly wire, and wrap one end around the base of the loop units, 2 or 3 times tightly. Cup and flute each of the 6 round petals, right side in, and add them, one at a time, right sides up, around the base of the loop units. Wrap the assembly wire, twice, tightly, with each addition. Add 5 green sepals in the same way but with the wrong sides in. Cut off and thin out the excess petal and calyx wires, and cover the exposed wires with tape. Bend the head of the flower forward, and cup loop units inward.

Assembly of Bud

Balance the wires of the loops, and twist the wires together in the center of the underside of the loops. Tape them, and mount them to the top of a taped 16-gauge wire. Attach a piece of assembly wire to the base of the loops, cup the loops inward, attach the calyx, right sides out, one at a time, around the base of the loops. Cup the calyx around the loops. Cut off excess calyx wires, leaving only 1" or so, and cover them with tape.

Assembly of Leaves

Twist together the bottom wires of the leaves and tape them individually. Combine 3 large ones with tape, and on each outer side, tape on one small leaf. Repeat with the remaining 3 large and 2 small leaves.

Four inches below the base of the flower, tape on a group of 5 leaves to the flower stem, and 1" below, tape on the bud stem, allowing 3" of stem on the bud. One inch lower, add the 2nd grouping of 5 leaves, and tape to the bottom of the stem.

Flower, 1-1/3" x 1¾".
Spray, 9" x 4".
See also color plate 2.

PETUNIA (*Petunia hybrida*)

The petunia is similar to the morning glory in technique, but the blossom has a much deeper throat and a wider bell shape at the top. Its natural colors range from pure white to deep violet, red and blue.

Materials for one cluster (4 flowers, 10 leaves)

Beads: 4 strands white; 12 strands blue; 10 strands green; ½ strand yellow

Wires: 24-gauge for the frame; 30- or 32-gauge spool; 26- or 28-gauge for leaves; 18-gauge for stem

Flower

To make the frame for the flower, cut 6 pieces of 24-gauge wire 4"
long. Stack them so that they are even at the bottom, and twist
the 6 wires together at one end for no more than 1". Transfer 1
strand of white beads to a spool of 30- or 32-gauge wire. Attach
the open end of the wire to the top of the twisted wire. Fig.
101. Open the 6 wires so that they are no more than ¼" apart at
the base. Treat each rib of the frame as a basic wire, and put 2
beads between each one, wrapping bare spool wire over and around
each rib as you work. Be sure to cross over the top of each rib, then
down and around. This will give you a right side on the outside of
the frame. Work the first 3 rows with 2 beads between each rib, 3
rows with 3 beads between each rib, then 5 rows with 4 beads
between each rib. Allow 36" of bare spool wire and cut the wire
from the spool.

Onto this wire, feed 2 strands of a contrast color. Spread open the
ribs making sure they are evenly spaced, and continue with the new
color, using just enough beads between each rib to fill the space.
Reverse the position of the frame so that the twisted wires are at the
bottom, and the ribs form a sunburst at the top. Continue wrapping
bare spool wire over the top of each rib as you work the next 9 rows.
For a larger flute, work 3 more rows if desired, 12 rows in all.
When the desired number of rows have been completed, wrap bare
spool wire 3 times around the last rib, and cut away the excess close
to the rib wire. Cut off all bare rib wires, leaving only ¼" on each,
and bend these wire ends down the wrong side of the flute. Make 4.

Fig. 66

10 BEADS

CUT

CUT

1½"
BEADS

CUT

Flower Stamen

Prestring onto a spool of 26- or 28-gauge wire, 10 yellow beads,
2½" of green beads, and 10 yellow beads. One inch from the open
end of the spool wire, make a loop of the first 10 yellow beads.
Close the loop with 3 half twists so that the twists are close to the base
of the loop. Push 1½" of the green beads to the base of the loop,
make a basic loop with bare wire. Push the remaining 1¼" of green
beads to the basic loop, and make another 10 bead loop with the
remaining 10 yellow beads. Fig. 66. Trim off spool wire close to
the base of both loops, and cut open the basic loop at the bottom of
the loop. Twist both bottom wires together to the end. Insert 1
stamen in the center of each flower, and tape together the wires at
the base of the flower. Tape each flower to the top of a taped

18-gauge wire. Make 1 pair for each flower in yellow and green.

Leaves

Small. BASIC: 4 beads, pointed tops, round bottoms, 9 rows. Make 6, in green.
Large. BASIC: 4 beads, pointed tops, round bottoms, 11 rows. Twist the bottom wires together and tape them. Make 4, in green.

Coiled Tendrils

Each pair of tendrils needs 10″ of beads. After transferring the green beads to the spool wire, coil the open end of the spool wire 3 times around a needle or corsage pin. Push 5″ of beads to the coil, and make a basic loop with bare wire. Push the remaining 5″ of beads to the basic loop, and at the opposite end of the beads, coil the spool wire around the needle 3 times. Cut away the bare spool wire at both ends, close to the coil, cut open the basic loop at the bottom of the loop, and twist both wires together, then tape them. Fig. 67. Wrap both 5″ tendrils around a round pencil, one at a time, to spiral them. Make 2 pairs, in green.

Assembly of Cluster

The 4 petunias shown are made of 2 separate branches that have been combined. For each branch you will need 2 flowers, 2 pairs of tendrils, 3 small leaves, 2 large leaves and 3 stem wires (18-gauge), one for each flower and one for the leaves and tendrils.

Tape a 10″ piece of 18-gauge stem wire, and to the top, tape 1 small leaf with no stem showing. Tape down the stem for 1½″, add a pair of small leaves with 1″ of stem showing, and 1 pair of tendrils with no stem showing. One inch below, add a pair of large leaves with 1″ of stem showing, and the second pair of tendrils with no

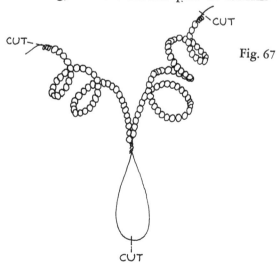

Fig. 67

stem showing. Two inches below the second pair of tendrils, tape on 1 petunia that has been taped to the top of a 6″ piece of 18-gauge stem wire. Allow 2″ of stem on the flower. Tape the second flower ½″ below the first one, allowing 1½″ of stem on the second flower. Make a second branch in the same way, and combine the two branches with tape ½″ below the two bottom flowers.

Flower, 1½″ in diameter.
Leaf, 2-1/3″ long.
See also color plate 17.

POPPY (Small)

One of the easiest flowers to make, this poppy is of the common garden variety. It is meant to resemble the one that grows so profusely in Flanders Field, and arranges well in small baskets.

Materials for one flower and two leaves

Beads: 2½″ strands red for 5 petals; 6″ black for stamens; 3 strands green for 2 leaves
Wires: 28-gauge spool; 18- or 19-gauge for stem

Petal

Two inches from the crimped end of the beaded spool wire make a narrow loop with 10 beads, wrap around the outer edge of the 10-bead loop with the beaded spool wire, create a 1-bead point, and secure the wraparound by wrapping bare spool wire twice around the wire at the base of the double loop. Wrap once again around the double loop, create a 1-bead point at the bottom, and secure the wraparound by wrapping bare spool wire around the bottom wire. Wrap around once more with beaded wire, creating a 1 bead point at the bottom. Allow 2″ of bare spool wire, cut the wire from the spool, and twist the two petal wires together for ½″. Fig. 10. Make 5 for each flower, in red.

Centers

Crimp the open end of the wire and 2″ from the crimped end, make

5 continuous loops, measuring 1¼″ of beads for each loop. Allow 2″ of bare spool wire and cut the wire from the spool. Give a half twist to the outer ¼″ of each loop. Make 1 for each flower, in black.

Leaf

Two inches from the crimped end of the beaded wire, make a narrow loop with 15 beads, wrap around the beaded loop with a row of beads, and secure the wraparound by wrapping bare spool wire around the bottom wire. Move 9 beads to the base of the double loop, and at the opposite end of the 9 beads create another narrow 15-bead loop and wrap around it once with a row of beads. Continue in this manner until there are 7 double loops, each one separated by 9 beads. Fig. 68. Allow 2″ of bare spool wire, and cut the wire from the spool. Fold the string of loops in half, and twist together the 2 end wires. Loops 1 and 7 should be opposite one another. At the base of the top loop, and between each pair of loops, give a half twist to the double row of beads to cross them, then tape the bottom wires together. Fig. 69. Make 2 for each flower, in green.

Assembly of Flower

Stack 5 petals, one on top of the other, right sides facing up, bottoms even, and twist the bottom wires together to form a stem. Slip the stem wires of 1 black center between any 2 flower petals, and tape together both sets of wires. One inch below the base of the flower, tape on a piece of taped 18-gauge stem wire (about 4″). Tape down the stem for 1¼″ and add a leaf to the left side of the stem. Tape down for a ½″ and add a second leaf on the right, then continue taping to the bottom of the stem.

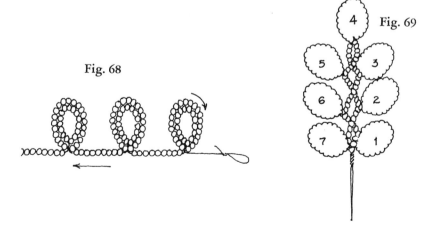

Fig. 68

Fig. 69

4″ x 4″. See also color plate 16.

PRIMROSES (*Primula*)

There are several hundred species of primroses in all shades, so any color choice is permissible. The flowers are of medium size and, clustered together, can be used alone in a small container or in a large bouquet as filler. These are in pale pink and white.

Materials for one cluster

Beads: 1 bunch pink; 1 bunch white; 1 bunch green
Wire: 26-gauge gold spool or 28-gauge silver

Large Flower

Make 5.
Unit 1. Make 12 continuous 12-bead loops, and allow 6″ of wire at both ends of the unit. Make 1 for each large flower, in pink.
Unit 2. Make 6 continuous 12-bead loops, and give each loop one wraparound after each 12-bead loop is made. Leave 6″ of bare spool wire at both ends of the unit. Fig. 10. Make 1 for each large flower, in white.
Unit 3. Make 6 continuous 15-bead loops, and give each loop two wraparounds after each 15-bead loop is made. Leave 6″ of bare spool wire at both ends of the unit. Make 1 for each large flower, in pink.

Small Flower

Make 6.
The small flower is made the same as the large one, but it uses only 1 Unit 1 and 1 Unit 2, eliminating Unit 3.

Large Calyx for Large Flower

Six inches from the open end of the spool wire, make a narrow loop of 1½″ of beads, close it loosely at the bottom by twisting the loop of beads once, only, to cross the wires at the base of the loop. Pinch off ¼" of beads—about 7 or 8—at the top of the loop, and give the loop of beads 1 full twist, thus crossing the wires at the base of the 7 or 8 beads and creating a loop. Bring beaded wire up the left side of the lower portion of the unit, wrapping bare spool wire around the base of the small 7-bead loop. Bead down the right side of the lower portion of the unit and wrap bare spool wire around the base of the unit. To the left of the unit just completed, repeat by making a second narrow loop with 1½" of beads, pinch off 7 or 8 beads at the top of the loop, cross the wires, and wrap beaded wire around the lower portion of the unit, the same as before. Fig. 70. Continue until 5 units have been completed. Allow 6" of bare spool wire and cut the wire from the spool. Make 5 (1 for each flower), in green.

Small Calyx for Small Flower

This calyx is made in much the same way as the larger one, but the wraparound is eliminated, and the measurement decreases to 1¼" of beads. Six inches from the open end of the spool wire, make a narrow loop of 1¼" of beads, pinch off the top 7 or 8 beads and twist the beads to cross the wires at the base of the beaded loop. To the left of the first loop, make another narrow loop with 1¼" of beads, pinch off the top 7 or 8 beads, etc. until 5 units (loops) have been made. Allow 6" of bare spool wire and cut the wire from the spool. Fig. 71. Make 6, in green.

Leaves

Two inches from the open end of the spool wire, make a narrow loop with 3" of beads, bead up the front of the loop, and down the back, then twist together the two bottom wires for ¼". Make 22 (two for each flower), in green.

Assembly of Large Flowers

Twist together the 2 wires of Unit 1 for 1" to form a stem. Set one Unit 1 in the center of 1 Unit 2, and twist both sets of wires for 1".

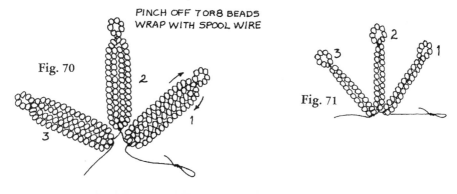

PINCH OFF 7 OR 8 BEADS
WRAP WITH SPOOL WIRE

Fig. 70

Fig. 71

Set the combined Units 1 and 2 in the center of 1 Unit 3, and twist all wires together for 1″. Set the combined flower units in the center of a large calyx and twist all wires together for 1½″. Add one leaf to the left of the flower stem, and 1″ below, add a second leaf on the right, then twist all wires together to the end. If silver wire is used, tape the flower wires with half-width tape, and tape on the leaves, one at a time, spacing them in the same way.

Assembly of Small Flower

Put the small flower together in the same way, and add 2 leaves to each.

All flowers have been mounted to the top of a short piece of taped 16-gauge stem wire. The stem wire should be no longer than the depth of the container to be used. The height of each flower is controlled by lengthening or shortening the flower stems as they are taped to the top of the 16-gauge wire. Cut away all flower wires that extend beyond the bottom end of the 16-gauge wire, and tape the stem all the way to the bottom. Curly fern, maidenhair fern and baby's breath may be added to the cluster of flowers also.

Spray, 6½″ x 4½″.
Each flower, 1½″ x 1½″.
See also color plate 2.

ROYAL CROWN FLOWER (*Calotropis gigantia*)

This flower derived its name in Hawaii because of the miniature "crowns" which form the center of the flower. Leis are made with the whole flower or the crown alone. Three full blooms are shown grouped to form a cluster. They grow in white and pale lavender; both have pale yellow centers.

Materials for one cluster

Beads: 1 bunch white; ½ bunch green; 1 strand yellow
Wires: 28- or 30-gauge spool for flowers and centers; 26- or 28-gauge for leaves; 18- or 19-gauge for stem

Flower

Each petal is made all on one wire. Create a basic of 4 beads, work 6 rows, round top and round bottom. The 6th row will finish at the top basic wire. Wrap the spool wire ⅓″ up the top basic wire and feed 6 beads onto the top basic wire. Make the top part of the petal with these 6 beads as the basic, and work 2 rows of beads on each side (5 rows in all) with a pointed top and round bottom. Fig. 65. Cut off all but ¼″ of the top basic wire and bend it down the wrong side of the petal. Wrap bare spool wire twice around this portion of the petal, to secure. Bring the bare spool wire down the wrong side of the round petal (the petal that was made first), and wrap the bare spool wire at the base of the round petal, finishing on the right side of the round petal. Push 2½″ of beads to the base of the round petal, fold the 2½″ of beads in half to form a narrow loop of beads. Twist the loop of beads twice to close the wires at its base. Give this loop a 4-row crossover by beading up the front and down the back of the loop. Secure the crossover row of beads by wrapping bare spool wire twice around the base of the loop. Allow 1½″ of bare spool wire and cut the wire from the spool. Reduce the bottom wires to 2 by cutting open one side of the basic loop close to the base of the petal. Twist both wires together for ½″. Make 5 petals to a flower, 15 petals for 3 flowers.

Centers

Two inches from the crimped end of the beaded spool wire, make a 6-bead loop, and wrap beads around the outside edge of the loop. Twist both wires together for ½″, allow 2″ of bare spool wire and cut the wire from the spool. Make 1 for each flower, in yellow.

Assembly of Flower

Stack 5 flower petals together, one on top of the other, right sides up, bottoms even, and twist all bare wires together to form a stem. Make sure you have the bottoms of the round petals close together. Form all petals into a circle, like a star, right sides up. Set a yellow center in the middle of the 5 petals, pressing it flat, and wrap its wires around the flower stem. Use ½-width tape and tape the flower stem. Shape the two part petals like a ball, with the pointed part of the petal pointing down. Roll (coil) the crossover loop upward

Fig. 65

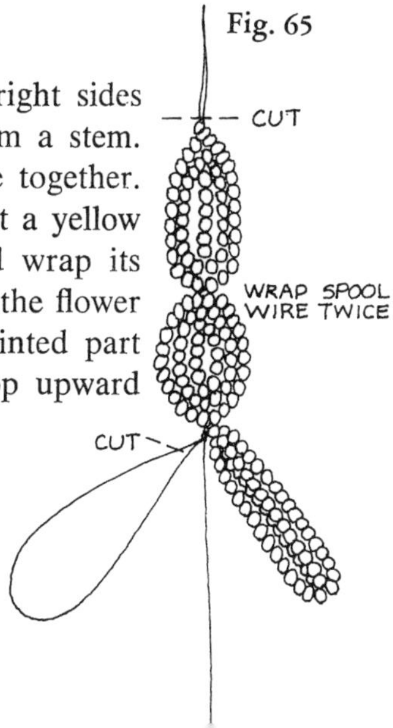

CUT

WRAP SPOOL
WIRE TWICE

CUT

for 1 full coil (about ½"). Tape each blossom to a taped piece of 18- or 19-gauge stem wire that has been cut 10 or 11 inches long. Combine the 3 stems with tape, 2½" below the base of the flowers.

Leaves (Green)

Small. BASIC: 5 beads, pointed tops, round bottoms, 5 rows. Make 3.
Medium. BASIC: 7 beads, pointed tops, round bottoms, 9 rows. Make 2.
Large. BASIC: 9 beads, pointed tops, round bottoms, 15 rows. Make 4.
Cover the bottom wires of the leaves with tape. One inch below the flowers, tape on 3 small leaves around the stem, no leaf stem showing. One-half inch lower, add the 2 medium leaves, one on each side of the flower stems. Show ½" on both medium leaves. One-half inch lower, add a pair of large leaves, and one-half inch lower, add the remaining pair of large leaves. Show ½" of stem on both pair of large leaves, and continue taping to the bottom of the stem wires.

Bend flower heads down, and shape the leaves as shown in the photograph.

Flowers, 3½" x 1¾".
Branch of three, 12" long.
See also color plate 8.

SHRIMP PLANT (*Beloperone guttata*)

This exotic, tropical flower is native to Hawaii, Mexico and southern United States. The orange-yellow color combination is the most prevalent; in Mexico, however, it grows in lavenders and pinks. The heartshaped petals (bracts) overlap one another to create the illusion of the curved tail of a shrimp. Four flower heads have been combined with clusters of small and large leaves to form this branch.

Other combinations have been used in the tropical arrangement in Color Plate 8.

Materials for one branch

Beads: 1 strand yellow; ½ strand white; 2½ bunches orange; 9 strands green for leaves
Wires: 26- or 28-gauge spool; 16-gauge for stem

Flower Petals

Unit 1. BASIC: 5 beads, pointed tops, round bottoms, 5 rows.
Reduce the bottom wires to 2. This unit can also be made, all in one, with a double split basic, if desired, by making the 2 yellow petals first. Create a basic of 5 yellow beads, and slip 5 yellow beads into the basic loop before closing it. Make a 5-row petal on the top 5 beads, push the remaining 5 beads to one side of the basic loop, cut open the loop at the bottom of the loop, and make another 5-row petal with the remaining 5 beads. Onto the other half of the basic wire, put 5 white beads. Allow 10″ of bare spool wire and cut the wire from the spool. Onto this wire put enough white beads to make the third 5-row petal. You will finish with one wire at the completion of the third petal. Trim off all top basic wires, as usual, and point all petals upward, wrong sides in. Make 1 in white, 2 in yellow.
Unit 2. BASIC: 5 beads, pointed tops, round bottoms, 9 rows.
Make these petals the same as the smaller ones, but put 10 beads into the basic loop before closing it, build the first petal on the original 5 bead basic, then put 5 beads on each side of the basic loop before cutting it open at the bottom of the loop. Crimp both open ends of the basic loop after it has been cut open, so that the basic beads won't slip off. Create a petal around each of the 5 beads, one at a time. You will finish with one wire. Fig. 25. Make 5 sets of 3 petals each, in orange, using double split basic technique.

Leaves

Small. BASIC: 4 beads, pointed tops, round bottoms, 9 rows.
Curve the basic wire slightly to the right as you make each leaf. Cut open the basic loop at the bottom of the loop, and tape all 3 wires together to form stems. Make 5.
Large. BASIC: 4 beads, pointed tops, round bottoms, 11 rows.
Curve the basic wire to the right, cut open the basic loop at the

bottom of the loop, and tape all 3 wires close together to form stems. Make 9.

Assembly of Branch

Tape four 16-gauge wires, individually, and cut them 12″ long. To the top of each wire, tape on 1 Unit 1. Tape down the stem for 1″ and add one Unit 2 so that its petals encircle the 3 petals of Unit 1. Point the petals upward. Tape down the stem for ½″ and add a second Unit 2 in the same manner, shaping the 3 petals upward. Add the next 2 Unit 2's, ½″ apart, tape down the stem for 1″, and add a small leaf to the left. Tape down 1″ and add a large leaf to the right. Leave 1½″ of stem on all leaves.

Assembly of Cluster

When all three wires have been trimmed with flowers and leaves, combine the 3 branches by taping them together at the bottom of the leaves. Tape down the combined stems for 1½″ and around the stems add 5 large leaves and 1 small leaf allowing ¾″ of stem on all leaves. If this cluster is to be the highest in the arrangement, the stem may need reinforcing with another piece of 16-gauge wire. If so, add it under the bottom leaves.

8″ long. See also color plate 18.

SILVER DOLLARS (*Lunaria annua*)

The silver dollar plant has several other common names, for example, Honesty and the Money plant. Its seed pods, when dried, are paper thin, and are used extensively for dried arrangements. Choose a translucent bead for these, (alabaster, opaline) and edge them in a contrast color (butterscotch or deep gold).

Materials for one stalk

Beads: 5 strands soft white; 2 strands butterscotch or deep gold
Wires: 26-gauge gold spool; 16-gauge for stem
Work with a very long basic loop, about 12″, and a generous top basic wire, about 6″. There are two sizes on the stalk, 4 small discs and 6 large discs. For longer stalks, make more of each size.

Small Disc

BASIC: 4 beads, round tops, round bottom. Rows: 9 in white, 10 and 11 in butterscotch. At the completion of the 9th row, allow 10″ of bare wire and cut the wire from the spool. Feed on enough beads in a contrast color to work the 10th and 11th rows. On the top basic wire put enough white beads to bead down the wrong side of the disc. Cut open the basic loop at the bottom of the loop, and twist all 4 wires together for 1″. Make 4.

Large Disc

BASIC: 4 beads, round top, round bottom. Rows: 11 in white, 12 and 13 in butterscotch. At the completion of the 11th row, cut off the spool wire, allowing 10 to 12 inches, feed on the contrast color and work rows 12 and 13. Put white beads on the top basic wire and bring it down the wrong side of the disc, the same as for the large disc. Make 6.

Assembly of Stalk

Combine 2 small discs by twisting their wires together for ½″, 1″ below the discs. Cut and cover a 16-gauge stem wire with tape. The length of the wire will depend on how long a stalk you wish to make. For the stalk shown, a 12″ piece is sufficient. To the top of the stem wire, wrap the untwisted portions of the first 2 discs for ½″ down the stem. To the right side of the stem, wrap the untwisted wires of the 3rd disc for ½″. To the right of the stem, wrap the untwisted wires of the 4th disc, etc., until all discs have been added to the main stem. You will be gathering more and more wires as you wrap. Arrange them so that they form a flat ribbon effect around and down the 16-gauge wire. Cover the last 2″ of wire with tape to secure them to the main stem.

Flower, 1⅝" x 1".
Spray, 7" x 5".
See also color plate 9.

SNOWFLAKES (*Leucojum vernum*)

The nodding heads of the snowflake form a graceful crown in the bouquet of miniatures, Color Plate 9. They are a very early spring flower, often pushing their way up through the snow. They grow only in pure white.

Materials for one cluster (4 flowers, 2 buds, 8 leaves)

Beads: 9 strands white; 7 strands green
Wires: 26-gauge silver or 26-gauge gold spool; 18-gauge for stem

Flower

BASIC: ¾", pointed tops, round bottoms, 5 rows.
Each flower has 6 petals, and the stems will be thinner if the petals are made using the double split basic method (see General Instructions chapter), and combining two sets of 3 petals each.

Working with at least 10" of wire in the basic loop, create a basic of ¾" of beads and put 1½" of beads into the basic loop. These 1½" of beads will be used for the basics on 2 other petals. Create a 5-row petal on the first ¾" basic, divide the 1½" of beads in the basic loop so that there are ¾" of beads on each side of the basic loop. Fig. 23. Cut open the basic loop at the bottom of the loop, crimp the ends of the wires so as not to lose the beads, and build a 5-row petal on each wire, thus finishing with 1 wire for 3 petals. Allow 6" of bare spool wire and cut the wire from the spool. Make 8 sets for 4 flowers.

Buds

For each bud, make 1 set of 3 petals with the double split basic, and leave 5" of bare spool wire, then cut it from the spool. Make 2 sets for 2 buds.

Calyx

BASIC: 4 beads, round tops, round bottoms, 8 rows.
Create a 4-bead basic with 10″ of wire in the basic loop, and 5″ for the top basic wire. For row 2 use 6 beads, insert a round pencil point between the 2 rows of beads to form a circle. Bend the top basic wire and the bottom basic loop wires down (as for beehive centers and strawberries) and continue building the calyx, using 8 beads for rows 3 and 4, 9 beads for rows 5 and 6, and 10 beads for rows 7 and 8, finishing at the top basic wire. Allow 5″ of bare spool wire, and cut the wire from the spool. Cut open the basic loop at the bottom of the loop, thus giving the calyx 2 wires at both ends. Twist together each pair of wires and insert both sets of wires into the center of the calyx and out through the hole in the top; thus it becomes the bottom of the calyx. Make 6, 1 for each bud and 1 for each flower, in green.

Assembly of Flower

For each flower combine 2 sets of 3 petals by stacking them, wrong sides in, bottoms even and twisting the bottom wires together to form a stem. Shape the petals into a bell, flair out the pointed ends, and attach a calyx to the base of each flower by inserting the flower stems into the center of the calyx. Push the calyx up close to the base of the petals, twist both sets of wires together firmly and tape them.

Assembly of Bud

Using a set of 3 petals for each bud, shape them the same as for the flowers and add a calyx to each bud. If gold wire has been used, no taping is necessary on the stems. Just twist the wires firmly, all the way to the end.

Leaves

Small. BASIC: 2″, pointed tops, round bottoms, 5 rows. Make 6, in green.
Large. BASIC: 2½″, pointed tops, round bottoms, 5 rows. Make 2, in green.

Assembly of Cluster

Cut 2 pieces of 18-gauge stem wire 6½″ long, 2 pieces 4″ long, 2 pieces 3″ long, and tape them. To the top of the 4 longest wires tape 1 small leaf with no stem showing, and 1 flower with 1½″ of stem showing. To the other 2 wires tape 1 small leaf, no stem showing, and 1 bud with 1½″ of stem showing. Stack all stem wires so that they are even at the bottom and tape all 6 wires together 2½″ up from the bottom, then tape on the 2 large leaves where the 6 stems are joined. Curve the flower heads and buds down and shape the leaves.

Flower, 5½″ in diameter.
See also color plate 5.

SPIDER MUMS

Of the many kinds of chrysanthemums, this one is, by far, the most fascinating. Its exceptionally shaggy appearance sets it apart even from other mums. It lends itself well to all types of bouquets, but is particularly well suited to Oriental arrangements.

Materials for one

Beads: 1 bunch for flower and bud; ½ bunch green
Wires: 26-gauge spool; 14-gauge stem for flower; two 16-gauge stem for leaves

Flower

There are 7 units to the flower. The first 3 units are made with continuous loops. They can be the same color as Units 4, 5, 6 and 7 or can be worked in soft yellow or pale green. Those shown are all white.

Unit 1. Make 10 continuous loops, measuring 1½″ of beads for each loop. Make 1.

Unit 2. Make 15 continuous loops, measuring 2″ of beads for each loop. Make 1.

Unit 3. Make 18 continuous loops, measuring 2½″ of beads for each loop. Make 1.

Units 4, 5, 6 and 7 are coiled end tendrils using the same method as for the stamens in the morning glory, meadow rue, etc. All of the units are made in the same way, but the measurements increase.

| 1 | 2 | 3 | 4 |

Unit 4. Wrap the open end of the beaded spool wire around the pointed end of a darning needle or corsage pin three times. Push the wraps close together to form a coil. Remove the needle or pin, move 1½" of beads to the coil. At the opposite end of the 1½" of beads, make a basic loop so that the beads fit snugly between the coiled end and the basic loop. Move another 1½" of beads to the basic loop, and make a coil of 6 wraps with the bare spool wire. Cut in between the wraps of wire. This constitutes one pair of tendrils. Make 6 pairs and cut open the basic loop at the base of the loop. Fig. 59.

Unit 5. On each pair, increase to 2" of beads on each tendril. Make 9 pairs.

Unit 6. On each pair, increase to 2½" of beads on each tendril. Make 9 pairs.

Unit 7. On each pair, increase to 3¼" of beads on each tendril. Make 14 pairs.

Bud

Make 2 pairs of Unit 4 for the bud.

Flower Calyx

BASIC: 12 beads, round top, round bottom, 12 rows.
Create a 12-bead basic, and use 12 beads for row 2. Wrap bare spool wire twice, around the top basic wire for extra security. Insert a round pencil between the 2 rows of beads to form a circle. Wrap around the circle of beads with beads, securing top and bottom, until there are 6 rows of beads on each side—12 rows in all. Fig. 42. Cut open the basic loop at the bottom of the loop. This will give the circle of beads 2 wires at both ends. With the wrong side of the calyx facing up, bring both sets of wires to the middle, and through the center hole to the right side of the calyx. Make 1, in green.

Bud Calyx

Make 7 continuous loops, measuring 3" of beads for each loop. Skip-lace the loops through the center and close the calyx by bringing the ends of the lacing wires together, wrong sides in, and twisting them together for ½". Cut away all but ¼" and tuck the remaining wire to the inside. Insert 2 pairs of Unit 4 petals into the center of the calyx loops, twist the bottom wires together to form a stem, and tape them. Make 1, in green.

Leaves

Create a basic of 1¼" and 5 rows, pointed top, round bottom. Make 2 loopbacks on each side of the center unit of 5 rows, the first pair as high as the top of the basic row of beads, and the second pair to the middle of the basic row of beads. Make the 1st loopback on the left, the 2nd on the right, the 3rd on the left and the 4th on the right. When securing loopbacks 1 and 3, cross bare spool wire in front of the bottom basic loop, to the back of the leaf, and bring it forward to the right of the loop being made. Loopbacks 2 and 4 have normal wraps at the bottom. Make 6. Fig. 11.

Assembly of Flower

Balance the end wires on Units 2 and 3. Twist together the end wires on Unit 1 to form a stem, and insert the stem into the center of Unit 2. Twist both sets of wires together, and insert them into the center of Unit 3, then twist the 3 sets of wires together. Cut away all but 1½" of the wires and tape them. Tape the combined units to the top of a 14-gauge stem wire, and attach a 30" piece of assembly wire to the base of the combined units, wrapping the wire 3 or 4 times to secure. With the assembly wire, add the pairs of Units 4, 5, 6 and 7 around the base of the loop units, wrapping twice, tightly, with each addition. When the last Unit has been added, wrap several times more, to secure, and cut away any excess assembly wire. Thin out the wires of all units, taper them and cover the exposed wires with tape. Insert the opposite end of the stem wire into the center of the calyx, and push the calyx up close to the base of the flower. Cover the exposed calyx wires with tape.

Assembly of Leaves

Tape the stems of all leaves, and to the top of a 9" piece of taped 16-gauge wire, tape one leaf, no stem showing on the leaf. Tape down the stem wire for 1½" and, on the left side, tape on another leaf, with ½" of stem showing on the leaf. Tape down for another 1½" and tape on the 3rd leaf, on the right side, with ½" of stem showing. Repeat with the other 3 leaves on another 9" piece of taped 16-gauge wire.

Five inches down the stem of the flower, tape on 1 leaf branch, on the left side. Tape down another 1" and add the bud, and 1½" lower, on the right side, tape on the 2nd leaf branch, then continue taping to the bottom of the flower stem.

Flower, 4½" in diameter.
See also color plate 3.

SPOON CHRYSANTHEMUM

Among the many varieties of "mums", one of the most unusual is the spoon mum, so called because of the disc at the end of each slim petal. Its colors are many, and it may be made all in one color, or in a combination of light and darker shades of the same color. The flower described here uses light- and dark-pink transparent beads.

Materials for one flower

Beads: 9 strands light pink; 7 ½ strands dark pink; 8 strands green
Wires: 26-gauge spool; 16-gauge for stem; 30- or 32-gauge spool for
*   assembling*

Flower

Unit 1. Make 10 continuous loops measuring 1½" of beads for each loop. Make 1, in light pink.
Unit 2. Make 15 continuous loops, measuring 2" of beads for each loop. Make 1, in light pink.
Unit 3. Make 18 continuous loops, measuring 3" of beads for each loop. This unit may be divided into 2 sections by making 9 continuous loops twice and joining the wires after the 2 parts have been completed. Fig. 72. Make 1, in light pink.
Unit 4. Crimp the open end of the beaded spool wire and move 1½" of beads to the crimped end. Three inches from the crimped end of the wire, make a 10-bead loop and give the 10-bead loop one wraparound with beads. Secure the wraparound by wrapping bare spool wire around the base of the double loop. Push the 1½" of beads to

2   1

WRAP SPOOL
WIRE

Fig. 72

the base of the wraparound loop, measure another 1½″ of beads to the first 1½″ of beads, and wrap bare spool wire twice around the single wire at the base of the 2 rows of 1½″ of beads. Measure another 1½″ of beads, and push them close to the base of the first 2 rows of beads. At the top of this third 1½″ of beads, make another 10-bead loop, and wrap around the 10-bead loop with a row of beads, and secure the wraparound by wrapping bare spool wire around the base of the double loop of beads. Measure another 1½″ of beads to the other 3 and twist the 2 bottom wires together. Allow 2″ of bare spool wire and cut the wire from the spool. This constitutes one pair. Make 5 more pairs in the same way, all in light pink. *Unit 5.* Repeat the design the same as for Unit 4, but increase the rows of beads from 1½″ to 1¾″. Make the wraparound loop the same size as before. Make 6 pairs, in dark pink.
Unit 6. Repeat the design the same as for Units 4 and 5, but increase the rows of beads from 1½″ and 1¾″ to 2″. Make the wraparound loop the same size as before. Make 8 pairs, in dark pink.

Make 2 pairs of Unit 4 for the bud, in pale pink, and combine them by twisting their bottom wires together to form a stem then tape the stem.

Calyx for Flower

BASIC: 12 beads, round top, round bottom, 10 rows.

Make a basic with 12 beads and use 12 beads for row 2. Wrap the bare spool wire around the top basic wire twice, to secure, and insert a round pencil between the 2 rows of beads to form a circle. Continue wrapping beads around the circle of beads until 10 rows have been completed. You will finish at the top basic wire, because there is an even number of rows. Allow 3″ of bare spool wire and cut the wire from the spool. Cut open the basic loop at the bottom of the loop, thus giving the calyx two wires at both ends. Bring both sets of wires to the wrong side of the calyx, and push them through the center circle to the right side of the calyx. Fig. 42. Make 1, in green.

Bud Calyx

Make 8 continuous narrow loops, measuring 1½″ of beads for each loop. Make 1, in green.

Leaves

BASIC: 1¼″, pointed tops, round bottoms, 5 rows, plus 2 loopbacks on each side (four loopbacks in all).

After the 5 rows have been completed, continue by bringing a loop of beads up the left side of the center section of 5 rows. Make this loopback as high as the top of the basic row of beads, using about 3¼″ of beads. To secure the loopback, cross bare spool wire in front, to the back and forward between the loop back and the center section of 5 rows. This raises the spool wire to the base of the 5 row section. Make a second loopback to the right of the center section, and have it the same height as the first loopback. Wrap the bare spool wire once around the bottom basic loop, normally. Create a 3rd loopback on the left, using only 2¼″ of beads, cross bare spool wire in front, to the back, and forward to the right of the loopback you are making (the 3rd). Make a corresponding loopback on the right, using 2¼″ of beads, and twist the bottom wires together. Allow 2″ of bare spool wire and cut it from the spool. Cover the leaf stems with tape. Make 6, in green. Fig. 11.

Assembly of Flower

Balance the wires of Units 1, 2, and 3, and twist together the bottom wires of Unit 1. Insert Unit 1 into Unit 2, and twist the bottom wires together. Insert the combined wires of Units 1 and 2 into Unit 3, twist all wires together, tape and cut away all but 1½″.

Tape a 16-gauge wire that has been cut to the desired length. Tape the combined Units 1, 2 and 3 directly to the top of the stem wire. To the base of the units, attach a 20″ piece of assembly wire, wrapping it 3 or 4 times to secure it firmly. One at a time, add the 6 pairs of Unit 4 around the base of the loop units, wrapping the assembly wire twice, tightly, with each addition. Add the 6 pairs of Unit 5, and the 8 pairs of Unit 6 in the same way, wrapping 3 or 4 extra times when the last pair has been added. Cut away any excess assembly wire, trim the petal wires at odd lengths, so as to slim the stem. Then cover all wires with tape. Insert the opposite end of the flower stem into the center of the wrong side of the calyx, pushing the calyx close to the base of the flower. Hold it securely with tape, tape down the stem for 1″ and cut away the excess calyx wires.

Assembly of Bud

Insert the wires of the bud stem into the center of the loops of the bud calyx. Push the calyx close to the base of the bud petals, and secure with tape.

Assembly of Leaves

To the top of a taped 16-gauge wire, tape on one leaf. Tape down the stem for 1½″ and tape on a 2nd leaf on the left side of the stem wire. Tape down another 1½″ and tape on a third leaf on the right side of the stem wire. Allow ½″ of stem on each leaf. Repeat with the other 3 leaves on another piece of 16-gauge wire.

Three and a half inches below the base of the flower, and on the left side, tape on one branch of 3 leaves. Tape down for 1″ and tape on the bud. Tape down another 1″ and add the second branch of leaves on the right side of the flower stem. Tape the stem wires together all the way to the bottom.

5½″ x 3″. See also color plate 5.

STAR-OF-BETHLEHEM (*Ornithogalum umbellatum*)

The origin of the Star-of-Bethlehem has been difficult to trace, however the consensus of opinion seems to place it in the Near East. Legend claims that the star-shaped flowers represent the star that guided the Three Wise Men of the East to Bethlehem. The flower, grown by monks and nuns, now grows wild throughout Europe. In America there are several cultivated species, and one of them is described here. When cut and placed in water indoors, the entire stalk of buds will open within a few days. This pattern caught the stalk midway, in half bloom, as it seemed more adaptable to arranging bouquets. The flowers are white, but the buds range from pale green to medium green.

Materials

Beads: 3½ strands pale green; 8 strands medium green; 1 bunch white

Wires: 28- or 30-gauge spool; 16-gauge for stem

Unit 1. Make 4 continuous loops, measuring ½″ of beads for each loop. Make 2, in medium green.

Unit 2. Make 6 continuous loops, measuring ¾″ of beads for each loop. Make 2, in medium green.

Unit 3. Make 7 continuous 3-row crossover loops, measuring 1″ of beads for each initial loop. Make 2, in medium green.

Unit 4. Make 9 continuous 3-row crossover loops, measuring 1¼″ of beads for each initial loop. Make 2, in pale green.

Unit 5. Make 9 continuous 3-row crossover loops, measuring 1½″ of beads for each initial loop. Make 2, in pale green.

Keep the units in separate envelopes that have been marked Units 1, 2, 3, etc. It will make the assembly of the stalk much easier.

Flower Units

A. Buds. BASIC: 5 beads, pointed tops, round bottoms, 3 rows. Make 12 petals (for 4 buds with 3 petals each).

B. Buds. BASIC: 7 beads, pointed tops, round bottoms, 5 rows. Make 15 petals (for 5 buds with 3 petals each).

C. Open flowers. BASIC: 9 beads, pointed tops, round bottoms, 5 rows. Make 30 petals (for 5 flowers with 6 petals each).

Stamens

Prestring 2 beads in a contrast color (usually yellow), 10 beads in the petal color (usually white), and 2 more beads in the contrast color. Coil the open end of the spool wire around a needle or pin 3 times, keeping the coils close together. Push 2 beads of the contrast color and 5 of the petal color to the coiled end of the wire. At the opposite end, make a basic loop with bare spool wire, push the remaining beads to the basic loop, and coil the opposite end around the needle. Fig. 59. Cut away the spoolwire close to the coil at both ends. Cut open the basic loop at the bottom of the loop. Make a second pair and combine the 2 pair by twisting the bottom wires together. Make 10 pairs, 2 pairs for each flower.

Leaves

BASIC: 3″, pointed tops, round bottoms, 7 rows.

Lace the leaves, individually, once through the middle, right sides up. Make 2, in medium green.

Assembly of Buds

For the small bud, stack 3 petals, one on top of the other, wrong sides up, and bottoms even. Twist the bottom wires together for an inch or so, close to the base of the petals to form a stem. Swing the 3 petals into a triangle, then cup them out and up so that the pointed tops meet. Cover the stem wires with half-width tape. Combine the petals for the large bud the same way, and tape the stems.

Assembly of Flower

Stack 6 petals, right sides up, and swing the petals into a circle. Lift the petals up and out, and slide 2 pairs of stamens between two petals, and tape both sets of wires to form a stem.

Assembly of Stalk

Tape a 10″ piece of 16-gauge stem wire, and to the top of it, tape 1 Unit 1. Crush the 4 loops up, wrap twice around with tape, tear off tape, and cut away the wires of Unit 1 directly below the tape. Tape on the 2nd Unit and set it so that the top of the loops are half way up the loops of 1st Unit 1. Tape twice around, tear off tape, and cut away the wires of the 2nd Unit 1 directly below the tape. Balance the wires on all remaining units by backweaving one end wire half-way around the loops. (See General Instructions Chapter.) Add each new unit by inserting the open end of the stem wire into the center of the loops. Tape them on in the same way, so that the top of each new unit that is added is halfway up the preceding one. Be sure to cut away the wires of each unit after it is taped on. When all of the loop units have been added, tape on the smallest buds around the stem wire, allowing 1½″ of stem on each bud. Add the larger buds ½″ below and in between the smaller ones. Tape all 6 flowers 1″ below the larger buds, and allow 2″ of stem on each flower. Two inches below the flowers, tape on the 2 leaves, one on each side of the stem wire, then continue taping to the bottom of the stem. Curve the entire stem slightly.

TANSY (*Tanactum*)

Tansy is a wild flower often seen along the edge of country roads, although it is sometimes cultivated in herb gardens as well, since the leaves are used in cooking to season tea and puddings. It comes only in yellow. There are usually 25 to 30 small button flowers to a head, and they are grouped in 3's before being mounted on a master stem.

Materials

Beads: 6 strands yellow; 8 strands green
Wires: 28-gauge spool for flowers; 26-gauge for leaves and calyx;
* 16-gauge for stem*

Flower

Create a basic of 3 beads and 4 rows, round top and bottom. Bend the top and bottom wires down, and use 9 beads for rows 5 and 6, 10 beads for rows 7 and 8; 11 beads for rows 9 and 10 so that the rows of beads form a cap. Fig. 73. Work with a generous basic loop, as this wire will be part of the stem of the flower. Cut open the basic loop at the bottom of the loop. The flower will have 2 wires at both ends. Combine the 4 wires in the center of the wrong side of the flower and twist them together. Make 27, in yellow.

Fig. 73

Calyx

Make 6 continuous 12-bead loops, allowing 3" of bare spool wire at both ends of the calyx. Make 27, in green.

Assembly of Flower

Place a calyx at the base of each flower, so that the green loops encircle the flower. Twist both sets of wires together for ½", letting the remaining wires hang straight. Your stems will be neater if the

1   2   3   4   5

wires are not twisted all the way to the bottom. Using half-width tape, cover the combined wires. Still using half-width tape, combine the flowers in groups of 3's 1½″ below the bottom of the flowers. This will give you 1½″ of stem on each flower. Tape a 16-gauge wire that has been cut to the desired length (about 9″), and tape 12 flowers around the top of it so that the flowers form a cluster. Cut 3 more 16-gauge wires 7″ long, and to the top of 2 of them tape on 3 flowers. To the last one tape on 9 flowers.

Leaves

Large. Two inches from the open end of the beaded spool wire, make a narrow loop of 2″ of beads, bead up the front of the loop, and bring bare wire down the back of the loop, securing the spool wire by wrapping it around the base of the 3-row crossover loop. Move 8 beads to the base of the loop, and repeat the crossover loop at opposite end of the 8 beads. Move 8 beads to the base of the 2nd loop, and at the opposite end of the 8 beads, make a third narrow loop of 1½″ of beads. Give the loop a 3-row crossover, secure the crossover by wrapping bare spool wire at the base of the third loop, and push 8 beads to the base of the 3rd loop. Repeat at the opposite end of the 8 beads with another 3-row crossover loop using the same measurements (1½″). Move 8 more beads to the base of the last loop, and repeat another 3-row crossover loop using the same measurements (1½″). Move 8 beads to the base of the loop and make another crossover loop measuring 1″ of beads for this one. Repeat two more times for 2 more loops, each loop separated by 8 beads. Make 3 crossover loops with 1½″ of beads, and 2 with 2″ of beads, and separate each loop with 8 beads. Fig. 74. Fold the long line of loops in half, and twist the bottom wires together. Give one full twist to the double row of 8 beads between each loop, and shape the loops upward. Tape the stems. Fig. 75. Make 3, in green.

Small. Make the small leaf in the same way but make only one crossover loop using 2″ of beads, one using 1½″ of beads, 3 with 1″ of beads, 1 using 1½″ of beads, and one using 2″ of beads. Fold in half, twist bottom wires together, and give 1 full twist to the double row of 8 beads between each loop. Shape the loops upward, and tape the stems. Make 3, in green.

Fig. 74

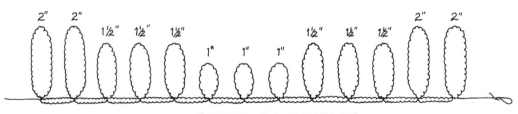

8 BEADS BETWEEN EACH LOOP

Assembly of Cluster

Tape one small leaf to the stem of the 12-flower cluster 3½″ below the base of the flowers. To the 2 three-flower clusters, add 1 small leaf each, 3″ below the base of the flowers. To the stem of the nine-flower cluster, tape one large leaf 3″ below the base of the flowers. Group all stem wires together so that the stems are even at the bottom, and tape them together, starting the tape at the base of the large leaf. Add the other 2 large leaves and tape to the bottom of the stems.

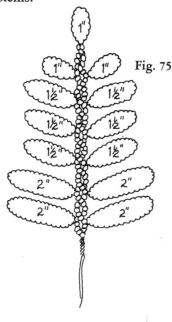

Fig. 75

Flower 1¾″ x 1¼″.
See also color plate 10.

TEA ROSES (*Rosa odorata*)

This long-stemmed tea rose boasts an elegance few other flowers attain. For use in a formal setting, it is unsurpassed.

Materials for one rose

Beads: 1½ strands light pink; 4 strands dark pink; 7 strands green
Wires: 26- or 28-gauge spool; 18-gauge for leaf stems; 12- or 14-gauge for flower stems

Flower

Small petal. BASIC: 12 beads, round tops, round bottoms, 7 rows. Make 2, in dark pink.
Large petal. BASIC: 12 beads, round tops, round bottoms, 9 rows. Make 4, 5 or 6, in light pink.

Reverse-wrap the spool wire at the bottom of the large petals, and reduce the bottom wires to 2.

Sepals

BASIC: 12 beads, pointed tops, round bottoms, 5 rows. Reduce the bottom wires to 2 on all sepals. Make 5 per flower, in green.

Leaves

BASIC: 6 beads, pointed tops, round bottoms, 11 rows. Cut open the bottom basic loop at the bottom of the loop, thus leaving 3 wires at the base of all leaves, and tape them together. Make 9, in green.

Assembly of Flower

Combine the 2 small petals by cupping them, wrong sides in, and embracing them by setting their edges, one inside the other. Fig. 76. Twist their bottom wires together and tape them to the top of a taped 14-gauge (or 12-gauge) wire; tape the 2 small petals. Attach one end of a 20″ piece of assembly wire to the base of the petals, and wrap it tightly 3 times around to secure. Shape the large petals by pressing your thumb into the right side of the center of each one. Make the indentation deep enough to cup each petal like a spoon. Roll the tops of the petals outward. With the assembly wire, add the large petals, one at a time, around the base of the 2 small petals, wrapping twice, tightly, with each addition of a petal. Let the top of the petal be your guide, and set the petals right sides facing in. Add the 5 sepals around the base of the petals in the same way, right sides in. When all sepals have been added, give the assembly wire an extra wrap or two, and cut away the excess. Trim off, and thin out some of the petal and sepal wires to taper them, then cover the exposed wires with tape. Curve the sepals out and down.

Fig. 76

Rose leaves grow in groups of 3s and 5s. Use no less than 3 groupings of 3 leaves each for each rose. For heavier foliage, use one grouping of 3 leaves, and 2 groupings of 5 leaves. Mount each grouping separately, on 16- or 18-gauge wires, cut 7 to 9 inches long; tape to the rose stem approximately 3″ apart, on alternating sides. Allow ½″ of stem to each leaf, and tape one to the top of the stem wire, tape down the stem for 1¼″, and tape the second leaf on the left. Tape down another 1½″ and tape the 3rd leaf on the right. Continue the pattern if 5 leaves are to be used.

7½″ x 2⅛″. See also color plate 19.

TI LEAVES

Ti leaves, dried or fresh, are startling because of their tremendous size and shape. Those shown in Color Plate 19 were designed to resemble the dried ones, and are used as a background for the dried wood roses.

Materials for one leaf

Beads: 1 bunch butterscotch or light topaz
Wires: 26-gauge spool; 24-gauge for basic (15″ for each leaf); 30- or 32-gauge lacing wire; one 7″ piece 16-gauge for reinforcing stem
Tape: twig or brown

Leaf

BASIC: 3½″, pointed top, round bottom, 33 rows.

If 24-gauge wire is available to you, cut a piece 15″ long, tape 4″ of it at one end, and use the 24-gauge wire for the basic by feeding onto the untaped end 3½″ of butterscotch beads. Perhaps not all of the small beads will fit on the 24-gauge wire, but it is worth the effort in order to have the extra support that the heavier wire will give to the center of the leaf. String at least 6 strands onto the spool of 26-gauge wire before starting the leaf. Attach the open end of the beaded spool wire to the taped end of the basic wire, and at the bottom of the basic beads, wrapping it several times to secure. Fig. 27. Create a leaf with 33 rows, and reverse wrap at the bottom of the

1   2   3   4   5

leaf if the leaves are going to be used in the dried arrangement in Color Plate 19, as the reverse wrap will show two right sides when it is curled forward. If they are going to be used upright, the reverse wrap is not necessary. Work the leaf through the 7th or 8th rows and, with the spool wire still attached, lace the leaf in 3 places; once through the middle, a third of the way up from the bottom, and a third of the way down from the top. Using the top of the leaf as a guide, lace right side up. Work the next 2 rows and lace them, the next 2 rows and lace them, etc. until the 33 rows have been completed. Secure the lacing wires' ends by wrapping each one, twice, tightly, around the lacing wire between the last and next to last rows of beads, then cut off the excess wire very close to the beads. When the 6 strands have been used, finish at the bottom of the leaf, cut off the spool wire, string the remaining 6 strands of beads, reattach the spool wire to the bottom basic wires at the base of the leaf, and continue making the leaf. To reinforce the bottom of the leaf, tape a 7″ piece of 16-gauge stem wire to the bottom leaf wires, allowing 2 or 3 inches of the heavy wire to extend part way up the back to the leaf. Lace the heavy wire to the leaf to secure.

Flower, 1½″ x 1″.
Cluster of three, 5″ x 4″.
See also color plate 19.

TULIPS (small)

Many times you'll feel the need of a small flower that makes a major impression, but that's easy and quick to execute. Five or seven of these tulips can be combined for an effective small potted plant, or they can complement the small iris, comparable in size. The beaded stems are optional.

Materials for three tulips and four leaves

Beads: 4 strands yellow; 2 strands white; 5 strands green; 1 strand black

Wires: 28-gauge spool; 18-gauge for unbeaded stems; 19-gauge for beaded stems

Flower Petals

BASIC: 12 beads, pointed tops, round bottoms, 7 rows.

If the tulip petals are to be tipped, work the first 5½ rows in yellow, allow 10″ of bare spool wire, and cut it from the spool. Feed on enough beads in white, or any contrast color, to finish the 6th row and the top half of the 7th row, then feed on enough beads of the original color to complete the 7th row. Skip lace all 4 petals together by catching the 1st row, the basic, last row, 1st row of 2nd petal, basic row, last row, 1st row of the next petal, basic row, last row, etc., and close the flower by twisting the lacing wires together after folding the petals in half, wrong side in. Cut off all but ¼″ of the lacing wire, and tuck it inside the flower. Make 12, 4 for each flower.

Stamen

The stamen can be made in solid black or in black and green. The two-color combination can be prestrung: 8 black beads, 1½″ of green, and 8 black beads. Make a basic loop of bare wire in the middle of the 1½″ of green beads and, with the black beads, make an 8-bead loop on top of the 2 green beaded wires. Fig. 66. Cut open the basic loop at the bottom of the loop, and twist the two wires together. Cut away the excess wires at the base of the 2 8-bead loops. If the stamen is to be worked all in black, make an 8-bead loop, push ¾″ of beads to the base of the loop, make a basic loop of bare wire at the opposite end of the ¾″ of beads, push another ¾″ of beads to the basic loop, and at the opposite end of the second ¾″ of beads, make another 8-bead loop. Cut off the wires close to the 8-bead loops, the same as before.

Leaf

BASIC: 2½″, pointed tops, round bottoms, 5 rows.
Tape the bottom wires together. Make 4, in green.

Assembly of Cluster

Insert the stamen wires through the center of the tulip, and twist both sets of wires together. If stems are to be beaded: using the large stem beads, hook a 19-gauge wire to the base of the flower and finish off as described in General Instructions chapter, under Beaded Stems.

If the stems are not to be beaded, the flowers may be mounted on taped 18- or 19-gauge stem wires. Your flowers will be easier to arrange if you group the tulips in threes, with 4 leaves attached 3″ below the base of the flowers. If the stems are beaded, bead for 3″ on the center tulip, and 2½″ on the other two. Join the stems with tape, at the base of the beading, and tape the leaves on, one at a time, around the stem, at the base of the beaded stems.

2¾″ x 1½″.

WHORL LEAVES

Whorl leaves consist of 3 or more leaves radiating from a single point. This one has 6, and it is shown on the bluets as a change from the longer loopy ones of the cornflower.

Materials for one leaf

Beads: 1½ strands
Wire: 26- or 28-gauge spool

Leaf

The leaf is made with 6 four-row crossover loops and a double-beaded stem, in green.

Crimp the open end of the beaded spool wire, and move 1½″ of beads to the crimped end. Four inches from a crimped end, make 6 four-row crossover loops, measuring 1½″ of beads for the initial loop. Be sure the initial loop of 1½″ of beads is narrowed before beading up the front and down the back of the loop, and crossover the top of the initial loop with bare wire. At the completion of the 6th loop, bring bare spool wire to the back of the loops, and forward between loops 3 and 4. Bead down to the bottom of the 1½″ of beads to form a double-beaded stem, and twist both wires together, tightly, so that the beads for the double stem are pushed up firmly to the base of the 6 crossover loops. Allow 2″ of bare spool wire, and cut the wire from the spool. Fig. 77.

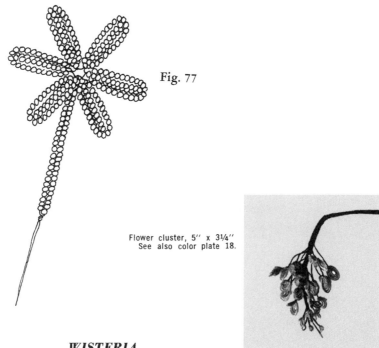

Fig. 77

Flower cluster, 5″ x 3¼″
See also color plate 18.

WISTERIA

Wisteria is a beautiful woody vine, with pea-like flowers in showy, drooping clusters. They grow in purple, yellow and white, and make an excellent low filler for large arrangements.

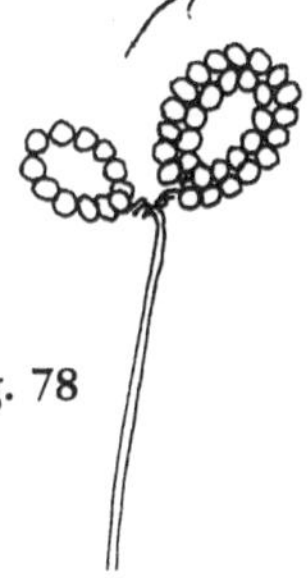

Materials for one cluster

Beads: 11 strands
Wires: 26- or 28-gauge spool; 18-gauge for stem

Flowers

Fig. 78

Leave 4″ of bare wire at both ends of all units.
Unit 1. Make 1 ten-bead loop. Make 1 for each cluster.
Unit 2. Make 2 continuous 10-bead loops. Make 3 for each cluster.
Unit 3. Make one 12-bead loop with 1 wraparound plus one 12-bead loop. Make 5 for each cluster. Fig. 78.

127

Unit 4. Make one 12-bead loop with 2 wraparounds plus one 12-bead loop with one wraparound. Fig. 79. Make 12 for each cluster.

Unit 5. Make one 12-bead loop with 3 wraparounds plus one 12-bead loop with one wraparound. Fig. 80. Make 15 for each cluster.

Make each wrapped row of beads close to the preceding row. Cup each unit so that the right sides of the loops face in, and cover the stem wires with half-width tape.

Assembly of Flower Cluster

Tape a 9" piece of 18-gauge wire. Add the flowers around and down the stem, starting with smallest unit on the top of the wire. Allow ½" of stem showing on Units 1 and 2; ¾" of stem showing on Unit 3; 1" of stem showing on Unit 4, and 1½" of stem showing on Unit 5. Curve the stem wire, and open the cluster of flowers by arching each one, up and out.

WISTERIA TREE

The wisteria tree shown in Color Plate 12 was built on a bare, dried manzanita tree, the small twigs were trimmed away, and the larger ones were cut for shaping. It was secured in a papier mâché pot with plaster of Paris. Plastic japonica leaves were added in all the desired places. Some were wired on with 22- or 24-gauge wire, others were taped on with brown flower tape. Last, the clusters of wisteria were added with tape, and the tree was set into the wooden tub. Florist sheet moss was used to cover the top of the container. There are 21 flower clusters on the tree which measures 5½ feet high and 4½ feet wide.

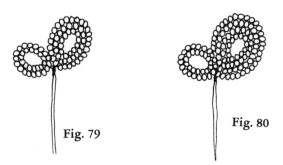

Fig. 79

Fig. 80

Diameter of large flower, 3½".
See also color plate 19.

WOOD ROSE (*Ipomoea tuberosa linnaeus*)

The wood rose is an intriguing flower. Its petals are pale beige on the inside, and mahogany brown on the outside. The "rose" is really the dried seedpod of a certain species of morning glory, and the 3 center petals hold the seeds. The original flower is yellow, but when it falls away, the calyx begins to open, dry, and become stiff and brown, thus the "wood rose". It is a great favorite in dried arrangements. There are 3 sizes shown in Color Plate 19 and they are merely a change in combination of the large and small petals.

Materials for one

Beads: 4½ strands light topaz or butterscotch; 6 strands brown
Wires: 26- or 28-gauge spool; 30- or 32-gauge for assembling, 16-gauge for stem

Petals

In order to achieve the light and dark, two-toned effect of the flower, the petals are repeated in both colors.

Large. BASIC: 6 beads, round tops, round bottoms, 17 rows.

For each rose, make 5 petals in the light color, and 5 in the dark color. Leave the top basic wire, and reduce the bottom wires to 2 by cutting open one side of the basic loop close to the base of the petal. Lace each petal, individually, across the center, right side up.

Small. BASIC: 6 beads, round top, round bottom, 11 rows.

For each rose, make 4 petals in the light color, and 4 in the dark color. Finish off each petal the same as for the larger ones, by leaving the top basic wire, and reducing the bottom wires to 2.

129

Center Pod

BASIC: 6 beads, round top, round bottom, 11 rows.

For each rose, make 3 in the lighter shade, and finish them in the same way by leaving the top basic wire, and reducing the bottom wires to 2.

Assembly of Flower

Combine the pod petals by stacking them, one on top of the other, wrong sides up, tops even, and twisting together the top basic wires. Cut away all but ⅓″ of the top twisted wires, and press them flat against the wrong side of the top petal. Swing the 3 petals into a circle. Bow out the petals to form a pod, bring the bottom wires together, and twist them to form a stem. Cover them with either brown or twig tape. Cut a piece of 16-gauge stem wire to the desired length, tape it, tape the base of the pod directly to the top of the stem wire, and set it aside.

Combine the small petals into 4 pairs, each pair consisting of 1 light and 1 dark petal. Join the 2 petals by stacking the 2 of them, right sides facing in, and twisting the top basic wires together. Cut off all but ⅓″ of the twisted wires, and flatten them against the wrong side of one petal. Reverse the petals so that the wrong sides face each other, twist the bottom wires together, and shape the petals as 1 petal, by cupping in the center, like a spoon. Roll the tops of the petals out and back, slightly, with the lighter petal in the inside (up). Combine and shape the other 3 pairs of small petals and the 5 pairs of large petals in the same way.

Use 30- or 32-gauge assembly wire for assembling the rose by attaching a 30″ piece of the wire to the base of the 3 pod petals that are mounted to the top of the 16-gauge stem wire. Wrap the wire 3 or 4 times, tightly, to secure. First add the 4 pair of small double petals, one pair at a time, around the base of the pod petals, wrapping twice, tightly, with each addition. Keep the base of these petals close to the base of the pod petals. Add the 5 double large petals around the base in the same way, and close to the base of the previously added petals. For extra security, wrap the assembly wire 3 or 4 times after the last pair of petals have been added. Add all petals with the light side facing up. Thin out and cut off at odd lengths the petal wires 1″ or so below the base of the flower. Cover the remaining exposed wires with brown or twig tape, and bend the head of the flower forward.

(Color plates are fully described on page 205.)

1. (Left) Boudoir lamps. 2. (Below) Royal Crown flowers with yellow mimosa; blue petunias and yellow tansy; calla lilies.

3. (Left) White foxgloves, spoon mums, lady bells and freesia. 4. (Below) A wedding assortment.

5. (Left) Chrysanthemums, star-of-Bethlehem, meadow rue. 6. (Below) Grapes with foliage. 7. (Opposite) Anthuriums, birds of paradise, and hosta leaves.

8. (Right) Shrimp flowers, hibiscus, and palmetto leaves. 9. (Below) A wedding "cake."

10. (Above left) Tea roses and baby's breath. 11. (Above) Peonies, bridal wreath, bachelor buttons. 12. (Below left) Wisteria tree. 13. (Below) Picture frame.

14. (Above left) Boston fern.
15. (Above) Hanging begonia.
16. (Left) Wrought iron spiral
steps. 17. (Below) Giant Matilija poppies; mountain bluets
and poppies.

18. (Above) Ginny roses, carnations, wisteria, tritoma, silver dollars and yellow gentians.   19. (Below) Varied groupings of dried and wild flowers.

20. (Left) Closeup of tree in plate 22. 21. (Below) Console lamps.

22. (Left) Christmas buffet table. 23. (Below) Ming tree.

The wood roses in Color Plate 19 show 4 as described, one small flower with 3 pod petals and 4 small pair, and one larger one with the 3-pod petals and 5 large pair.

12″ x 5½″. See also color plate 18.

YELLOW GENTIAN

Because the flowers surround the stalk, the gentian is an ideal flower to use in a two-sided arrangement (in place of, or with, delphinium, foxglove, tritoma, etc.).

Materials

Beads: 1½ bunches yellow for flowers; 3 strands pale green for stamens; 2 bunches dark green for leaves; 2 strands medium green
Wires: 28-gauge spool for flowers; 26-gauge spool for leaves; 14- or 16-gauge for stems

Flower

Petals. There are 6 petals to each flower and they are made with a double-split basic. Create a basic with 10 beads, and slip 20 beads into a generous basic loop. Give the 10 bead basic 5 rows, with a pointed top and round bottom. Turn the petal upside down, divide the 20 beads in half, so that there are 10 beads on each side, and cut open the basic loop at the bottom of the loop. Crimp both open ends, and create a 5-row petal on each of the 10 beads, working one at a time, thus making 3 petals all at one time and on 1 wire. You will finish with one wire. Allow 3″ of bare spool wire, and cut the wire from the spool. Trim off top basic wires normally. Make 2 sets of 3 petals each for each flower, 24 in all. Figs. 23, 24.

Centers

Unit A. BASIC: 10 beads, pointed tops, round bottoms, 3 rows. Make

3 for each of the 12 flowers in medium green.

Reduce the bottom wires to 2 and do not cut off the top basic wire. Stack the 3 green petals, one on top of the other, right sides up, tops even, and twist together the 3 top basic wires. Trim off all but ⅓″. Shape the petals by bending all of them down, wrong sides in, and twisting the wires together. Tuck the ⅓″ of twisted wire to the inside of the 3 petals. Fig. 81.

Unit B. One inch from the open end of the beaded spool wire, make a 6-bead loop. Push 1″ of beads to the base of the beaded loop, and at the opposite end of the 1″ of beads, make a basic loop. Push another 1″ of beads to the basic loop, and at the top of the second 1″ of beads, make another 6-bead loop. Make certain that the twists at the base of the 6-bead loops are tight, and cut away the bare wires very close to the base of the beaded loops. Fig. 66. Cut open the basic loop at the bottom of the loop, and twist both wires together. This constitutes one pair. Make 2 pairs for each flower (24 in all), in pale green.

Assembly of Flower

To the base of 1 Unit A, attach 2 pair of Unit B by twisting both sets of wires together to form a stem.

Combine both sets of yellow petals by stacking them face to face, right sides in, bottoms even, and twisting both bottom wires together. Slide the combined center units between 2 of the yellow petals and twist all bottom wires together to form a stem. Tape the stem and shape petals up and out and around the center units.

Leaves

BASIC: 1″, pointed tops, round bottoms, 15 rows. Twist the bottom wires together and tape them. Put a deep cup in each leaf with

Fig. 81

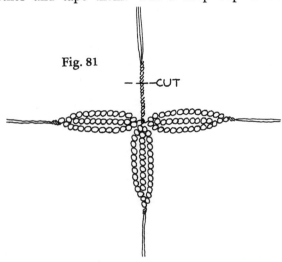

your thumb, and bend back the tops slightly. Make 12, in green.

Assembly of Flower Stalk

Use either one 14-gauge stem wire at least 14″ long, or 2 16-gauge wires, 14″ long, taped individually, then taped together, side by side.

To the top of the stem wire, tape on 3 flowers with ¾″ stems. Directly under the 3 flowers, tape on 2 leaves, right sides up, and directly opposite one another. No leaf stem showing. Tape down the stem for 2″ and around the stem, tape on 4 flowers with ¾″ stems. Under the 4 flowers, tape on 2 more leaves, the same as before. Repeat 2″ lower with 3 flowers and 2 leaves. Repeat 2″ lower with 2 flowers and 2 leaves. One inch lower, add another pair of leaves, and 1″ lower, add the last pair of leaves, all right sides up and directly opposite one another, then tape to the bottom of the stem.

III MINIATURES

Cluster, 3½" x 3".
Flower, 1½" x 1".
See also color plates 9, 13.

ARUM (*Miniature wild lily*)

This small English lily is shown in orange, but its natural colors include yellow, pale green, and white. The leaves are green, naturally.

Materials for one cluster (*8 flowers, 10 leaves*)

Beads: 3 strands orange; ½ strand yellow; 4 strands green
Wire: 26-gauge gold or silver spool

Flower

Fig. 82

BASIC: 8 beads, pointed top, round bottom, 7 rows. When row 7 has been completed, wrap bare spool wire around the base of the petal twice, allow 3" of bare spool wire, and cut the wire from the spool. Onto the 3" of bare spool wire, put 1" of beads in a contrast color to form the stamen. Push the 1" of beads to the bottom of the petal, and at the opposite end of the 1" of beads, coil the bare wire twice around a needle. Remove the needle and cut away the uncoiled wire. Fig. 82. Cut open the basic loop at base of the loop. If gold wire has been used, twist the wires together tightly to form a stem. If silver wire was used, cover the stem wires with half-width tape.

Leaves

Fig. 83

BASIC: 8 beads, pointed top, round bottom, 5 rows.

At the completion of the row 5, make a loopback of beads on the left of the leaf, then make a second loopback on the right of the leaf. Both loopbacks should reach to the middle of the basic row of beads. Fig. 83.

There are 8 lilies and 10 leaves shown in the cluster, and they are mounted to the top of a short piece of 18-gauge wire. The stems of the flowers and leaves vary in length from 1 to 2½ inches.

134

3¼″ x 3″. See also color plate 13.

BEADED BASKET

A white one to be filled with strawberries and carried to the hostess at a garden party.

Materials

Beads: approximately 8 strands
Wires: 24-gauge for frame; 30- or 32-gauge spool

Cut 7 pieces of 24-gauge wire 4″ long, and 2 pieces 15″ long. Stack them so that they are even at one end, and twist all wires together for ½″. Arrange the wires like the ribs of an umbrella, keep the 2 long wires together, side by side, and point the twisted wires down. Treat the 2 long wires as one rib until the basket is finished. Figs. 84, 84a. These 2 wires will then become the handle. Transfer 7 strands of beads to a spool of 30- or 32-gauge wire, and attach the open end of the spool wire to the twisted wires of the frame. Fig. 85. Starting at the base of the 2 long wires, put 2 beads between each rib, wrapping bare spool wire over and around each rib. This will make the 1st row. For the 2nd row of beads, use 3 beads between each rib; for the 3rd row, 4 beads; for the 4th row, 5 beads; and for the 5th and 6th rows, use whatever amount fills the space between the ribs. Keep these first 7 rows flat. After the 7th row, bend all rib wires down, so that they are parallel to the twisted wires. Fig. 86. Work 11 more rows, and turn the basket right side up. Bend the ribs at right angles to the sides of the basket, and work 7 more rows, flat, to form the outer rim. At the completion of the last row (there should be 25 in all), wrap bare spool wire 3 or 4 times around the last rib, close to the beads, and cut away the excess. Cut off all but ¼″ of the rib wires, and bend them down the back of the beaded rim. Onto each of the long wires, transfer 9″ of beads and secure them at the open end by twisting the bare wires together 3 times, close to the beads. Cut one wire off, close to the twists, and spiral the 2 beaded wires. Attach the single wire of the handle to the

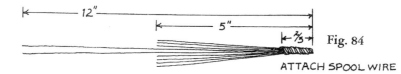

Fig. 84

ATTACH SPOOL WIRE

opposite side of the basket by wrapping it around the opposite rib between the last 2 rows of beads. Wrap it twice, then cut away the excess. Fill the basket with 6 or 7 red strawberries.

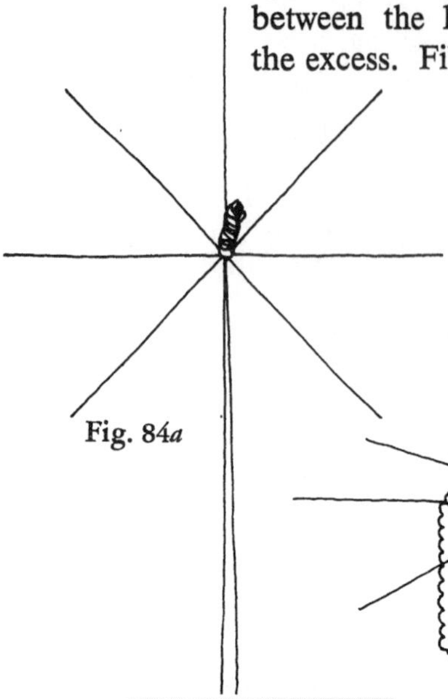

Fig. 84a

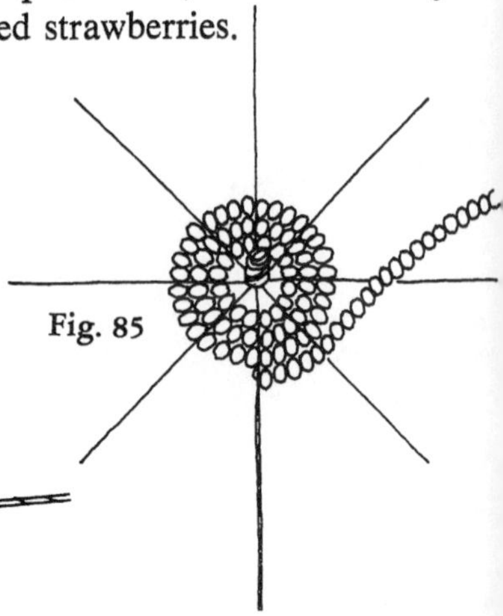

Fig. 85

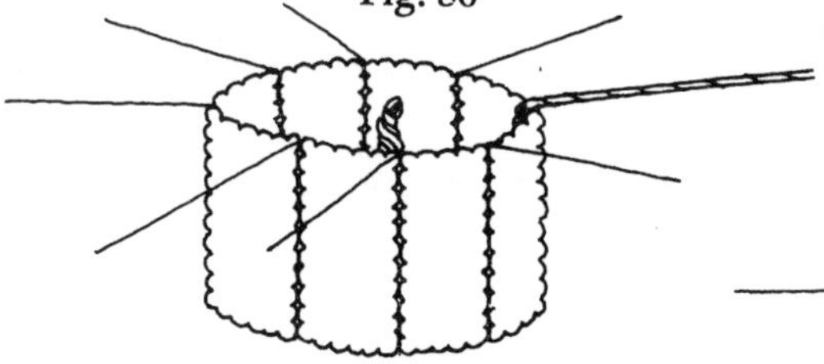

Fig. 86

Fig. 87

' x 2¾''. See also color plate 13.

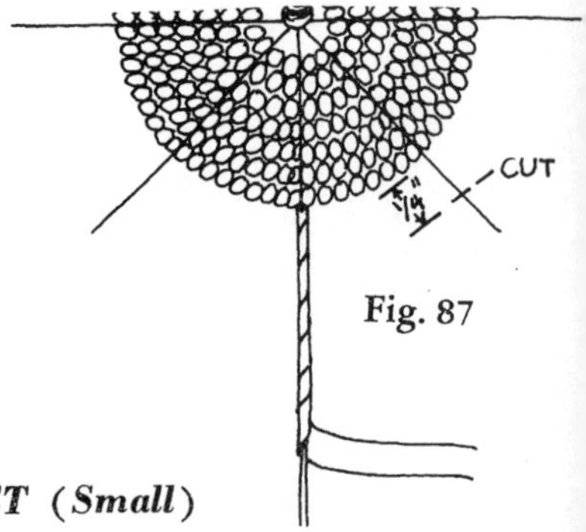

BEADED BASKET (Small)

This basket, shown in several ways in Color Plate 13, can also be filled with a nosegay of miniature flowers. It has been patterned from large cutting baskets and fireside baskets that are used for storing fireplace logs. A perfect gift, it is charming in green, white, yellow or light topaz (to resemble wicker).

Materials

Beads: 7 strands
Wires: 24-gauge coil for frame; 30- or 32-gauge spool

Basket

To make the frame for the basket, cut 9 pieces of 24-gauge wire so that there are 7 pieces 5″ long and 2 pieces 12″ long. Stack them so that they are even at the bottom, and at the bottom, twist all wires together for ⅔″. Figs. 84, 84a.   Use 2 pliers so that the wires are twisted tightly. Transfer at least 6 strands of beads to a spool or either 30- or 32-gauge wire, and attach the open end of the beaded spool wire to the frame ⅔″ from the bottom (where the twisting of the frame begins).

Open the frame wires to form a web, keeping the 2 long wires side by side, 3 wires to the left, one wire opposite, and 3 wires to the right, like the spokes of a wheel. Fig. 85. With the twisted wires of the frame pointing upward, wrap bare spool wire around the base of the 2 longest wires, crossing the spool wires over the top and around the 2 wires. To create the 1st row of beads, put 2 beads between each rib, wrapping bare spool wire around each rib as you come to it, working counter-clockwise. For row 2, put 3 beads between each rib, wrapping bare spool wire around each rib as you come to it. For row 3, put 4 beads in between each rib. It's important to wrap the spool wire over the top and around each rib. Be consistent as this will keep a decided right and wrong side to your work. After the completion of the third row, it is not necessary to count the number of beads placed between each rib. Just fill in the spaces between the ribs, and keep the ribs evenly spaced. Continue beading around the frame until 18 rows of beads have been completed. Make sure you finish at the long double wires, and wrap the spool wire around the double wires 3 times to secure. Treat the 7 short wires like top basic wires by cutting away all but ¼″ of the wire on each spoke, and bending it down the wrong side of the basket. This completes the basket. The 2 long wires are for the handle. Starting at the last row of beading, tape together the 2 long wires for 6″. Fig. 87. Wrap the beaded wire around the 6″ of taped frame wire. At the completion of the 6″ of beading, wrap bare spool wire 3 or 4 times to secure, and cut off the excess. This finishes the handle of the basket. To secure the handle to the opposite side of the basket, cut away 1 wire close to the beading. Insert the remaining wire to the left of the opposite rib, and between row 17 and 18 of beads. Cross the wire under this rib and bring the wire up between row 17 and 18 on the right of the rib. Wrap the wire around the base of the handle 3 or 4 times to secure, cut away any excess wire, and tape the center wires of the frame. Roll up the sides of the basket slightly to give it shape, and use a small piece of clay or styrofoam to hold the flowers in place.

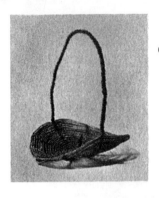

6¾" x 6". See also color plate 19.

BEADED BASKET (Large)

This basket is made exactly like the smaller one except that it takes one full bunch of beads and the frame is made with longer pieces of 24-gauge wire. It is shown filled with asters in Color Plate 19.

Basket

Cut 7 pieces of 24-gauge wire 7" long, and 2 pieces 18" long. Twist the wires together the same as for the smaller basket, add the beaded wire in the same place, use 2 beads for the 1st row, 3 beads for the 2nd row, 4 beads for the 3rd row, and continue putting beads between each row, using whatever amount is needed to fill the spaces between the ribs, and continue until you have completed 30 rows. Tape the two long wires together for 12½" (instead of the 6" used for the smaller basket), bead the handle for 12¼", and attach the handle in the same way, to the opposite side of the basket. Trim off all rib wires to ¼" and turn them down the wrong side of the basket.

3¾" x 2¼". See also color plate 13.

BEADED LOOP BASKET

Make this basket in several sections, which are joined together after all sections have been completed. Fill it with a cluster of any of the miniature flowers or, as shown, with 7 yellow-and-white miniature primroses and 8 shaded curly fern.

138

Materials

Beads: 1 bunch; 3 strands of contrast color are optional
Wires: 26-gauge silver spool; 30- or 32-gauge spool; 24-gauge for
handle and bottom rim

Basket Sides

Transfer at least 3 strands of beads to a spool of 26-gauge wire before starting, then make 19 continuous loops, measuring 3″ of beads for each loop. Allow 4″ of bare wire at both ends of the 19 loops. This is half of the basket, so repeat for the other half. Make these loop units close together at bottom of the loops. Skip-lace the top ¼″ of each loop, and lace each unit separately, fig. 88; set aside.

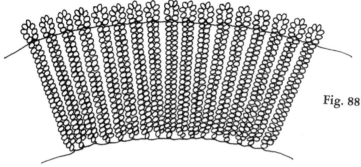

Fig. 88

Basket Handle

Cut a 9″ piece of the 24-gauge wire and tape it. Wrap it with beads that have been strung on 30- or 32-gauge spool wire. Start the wrapping 1″ from one end and wrap for 7″, thus leaving 1″ of unbeaded wire at the opposite end. Make 1.

Bottom Ring of Basket

Tape a 5½″ piece of 24-gauge wire, start the beading ½″ from one end, and bead for 4½″, thus leaving ½″ of unbeaded wire at both ends. Twist together both ends, and tape them. Form the beaded ring into an oval, pointing the ½″ of twisted wires toward the center of the oval. Make 1.

Basket Bottom

BASIC: 6 beads, round top, round bottom, 12 rows. Make 1.

The 12 rows of beads should be enough to fill the space at the bottom of the basket. However, leave enough wire and beads to make one more row of beads on each side (about 4″ of beads and 8″ of wire) before cutting the wire from the spool, just in case you need a 14-row bottom. Lace once through the middle, right side facing up, cut open the basic loop at the bottom of the loop, and leave all wires, as they will be used to attach the bottom of the basket to the sides of the basket. Fig. 89.

Assembly of Basket

Join the 2 loop units of the basket to form one long unit of 38 loops by twisting together one set of lacing wires and loop wires. Do not cut wires. A and B in Fig. 90. Using the lacing wires, attach one

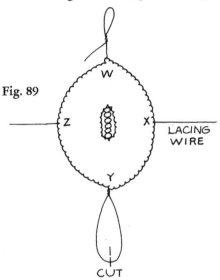

Fig. 89

end of the basket handle on the right side (at A) by wrapping the lacing wire around the taped wire at the base of the beading on the handle. Attach the other end of the handle in the same way at C, with the other end of the lacing wire. To close the basket, join wires E and C and D and F right sides in as in Fig. 90 and twist them together tightly. Turn back the top ¼″ of the loops, above the lacing, and cut off wires C and E, leaving only ¼″. Tuck this ¼″ of twisted wires under the top part of the loops and press flat against the lacing wires. Cut off all but ¼″ of the twisted D and F wires and push them to the inside of the basket.

Using the wires at the 4 "corners" of the basket bottom, attach the basket bottom to the bottom ring of the basket by wrapping each wire around the ring at w, x, y and z in Fig. 89.

Using these same wires, secure the basket bottom and ring to the bottom of the basket by wrapping twice more around the ring, but this time inserting the wires in through the looped sides of the basket, down through the bottom of the basket (twice in the same place with each set of wires). The wire may either be brought to the center of the basket, twisted together and pressed flat against the bottom of the basket or trimmed off close to the beads.

The handle and the bottom ring of the basket can be wrapped with 2 or 3 colors, if desired. Work with 2 or 3 spools of 30- or 32-gauge wire (one spool for each color) and wrap the 2 or 3 beaded wires at the same time.

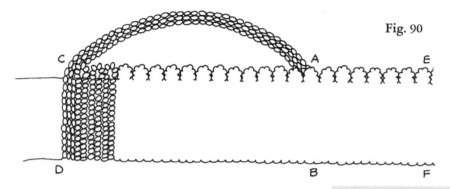

Fig. 90

Saucer, 3″ in diameter.
Cup, 1⅛″ x 1¼″.
See also color plate 13.

BEADED CUP AND SAUCER (*Miniature*)

This pattern may be increased to make a larger cup and saucer if desired. The technique is the same as for the beaded baskets.

Materials

Beads: 1 bunch
Wires: 24-gauge frame; 30- or 32-gauge spool

Saucer

Transfer 6 strands of beads to a spool of either 30- or 32-gauge wire. Cut 6 pieces of 24-gauge wire 2½″ long, stack them so that they are even at the bottom and twist all 6 wires together at one end for ½″. Open the wires into a circle so that they resemble the spokes of a wheel or the ribs of an umbrella. Attach the open end of the spool wire to the base of the twisted wires and wrap it several times to secure. With the twisted wires of the frame pointing upward, start at the base of one rib, wrap spool wire over and around twice. For the 1st row of beads, put 2 beads between each rib, wrapping over the top and around each rib. For the 2nd row, use 3 beads between each rib, and for the 3rd row use 4 beads. After the 3rd row, it is not necessary to count the number of beads used for the space between each rib. Use whatever amount it takes to fill the space and keep the ribs uniformly separated. Work for 18 rows, wrap bare spool wire around the last rib for 3 or 4 times to secure and cut the wire from the spool. Cut away all but ¼″ of bare wire on each rib, and bend it sharply down the wrong side of the saucer. Figs. 84, 84a, 85, 87.

Cup

Transfer another 4 strands of beads to the spool wire. Cut 5 pieces of the 24-gauge frame wire 3″ long, and 2 wires 5″ long. Stack them so they are even at the bottom, and twist them together at one end for ½″. With the twisted wires pointing downward, attach the beaded spool wire under the ribs at the top of the twisted wires. Arrange the ribs into a circle, evenly spacing the ribs. Keep the two longest wires side by side and twist them together for approximately 1½″. They will be treated as one wire (just as the long wires were for the handles of the baskets), until the sides of the cup have been completed. Start the beading at the double wire, and use 3 beads for the 1st row, 4 beads for the 2nd row, 5 beads for the 3rd row, and 6 beads for the 4th row. Keep these rows flat. Work 1 more row flat (5 rows in all) then bend the bare wires of the cup down so that they are parallel to the twisted wires. Fig. 86. Continue filling in the spaces with beads until 11 more rows have been completed, 16 rows in all. You will finish at the double wire. Wrap spool wire around the double wire 3 or 4 times close to the beads, to secure, and cut off the excess close to the beads. If the long wires are twisted beyond this point, untwist them back to the last row of beading. String beads on both wires for 3″. Twist the unbeaded wires together to secure, and spiral the beaded wires to form a handle. Bend the handle, to shape, bring bare handle wires across the bottom of the cup and up through the center. Set the cup on the saucer, and push the twisted wires of the saucer up through the center of the cup. Twist both sets of twisted frame wires tightly together with a plier, and cover them with tape. Fill the cup with a small piece of Styrofoam, or a small ball of clay covered with moss, and insert a cluster of miniature flowers—arum, thistle, wild flowers, etc.

Both cup and saucer may be edged with a contrasting color. For a larger size, increase to 20 rows for the saucer, and for the cup increase to 7 rows for the bottom of the cup, and 13 rows for the sides, 20 rows in all. Lengthen the handle by ¼".

¾" x 1". See also color plate 13.

BEADED FLOWER POT (For Miniature Hyacinth)

Fill this with the miniature hyacinth, or use other small flowers if you prefer.

Materials

Beads: 2½ strands
Wires: 24-gauge for the frame; 30- or 32-gauge spool

Flower Pot

Transfer 2½ strands onto the spool wire. Cut 6 pieces of 24-gauge wire 3½" long, stack them so that they are even at the bottom, and twist together at one end for ¾". Arrange the untwisted wires into a circle, like the spokes of a wheel or the ribs of an umbrella. Figs. 84a, 85. Wrap the open end of the spool wire 2 or 3 times around the base of the spokes (at the top of the twisted wires). Point the twisted wires downward (as for small cup), and starting at the base of one spoke, wrap bare spool wire once around, crossing over the top. Place 2 beads between this spoke and the 2nd one, cross bare spool wire over and around the base of the 2nd spoke. Put 2 beads between the 2nd and 3rd spokes and cross bare spool wire over and around the base of the 3rd spoke. Continue putting 2 beads between each spoke until 1 row of beads has been completed. For row 2 use 3 beads between each spoke, for row 3 use 4 beads between each spoke, for the remaining rows it is not necessary to count the number of beads in between each spoke. Use just enough beads to fill in the spaces between the spokes. Wrap for 6 rows, keeping the frame as flat as possible. This will make the bottom of the flower pot. At the completion of the 6th row, bend each spoke down to form the sides of the pot. Now continue filling all the spaces between the spokes for 11 more rows. This will be 17 rows in all. Keep the spaces even. Each space should take about 9 beads. When the last row has been completed, wrap the bare spool wire around the last spoke 2 or 3 times to secure it, and cut the wire from the spool. Cut off all but ¼″ of the remaining bare wires of each spoke, and bend the ¼″ of wire flat against the inside of the pot. Trim down the twisted frame wires if they protrude above the top of the pot. Press a small amount of clay or Styrofoam into the pot and insert the stem of the miniature hyacinth or any other small group of flowers.

Spray, 5¼″ x 6″.
See also color plates 13, 19.

BLUEBELLS *(Miniature)*

These sprigs of tiny bells are climbing on the beaded trellis. There are 3 branches, 2 with 5 bells and 6 leaves, and 1 with 7 bells and 10 leaves.

Materials for three branches

Beads: 5½ strands for flowers; 2 strands green for leaves
Wires: 26-gauge gold spool; short piece of 18- or 19-gauge for stem

Flower

Make 5 continuous narrow loops using 12 beads for each loop. Leave 4″ of bare wire at the beginning and end of all flowers, and twist the wires for 1". Shape the narrow loops up and then out to form small bells. Make 17.

Leaves

BASIC: 3 beads, pointed tops, round bottoms, 3 rows.
Reduce the bottom wires to 2 and allow 4" of bottom wires at the base of all leaves. Twist the wires for 1". Reduce the top basic wire to ¼", and turn down the wrong side of the leaf as usual. Make 22.

Assembly

The long wires on all of the flowers and leaves will enable you to join the sprigs together without having to mount them onto stem wires. Twist the stems of 2 leaves together for ¼", add a flower by twisting all wires together for ¼", add a leaf to the left and twist all wires together for ¼", add a leaf to the right and twist all wires together for ¼", etc. until you have completed a sprig with 7 flowers and 10 leaves. Make 2 more shorter sprigs with 5 flowers and 6 leaves. Group the 3 sprigs together with tape, setting the longer sprig in the center between the 2 shorter ones. Tape for 2" and cut away the excess wires. Mount on a 2" piece of taped 18- or 19-gauge wire, adding the stem wire to the taped portion of the combined sprigs. Wrap the taped wires for 1", with green beads that have been strung on 30- or 32-gauge assembly wire.

Flower, ½" x ½".
Cluster, 3½" x 2¼".
See also color plate 13.

CALLA LILY (Miniature)

Five of these tiny lilies have been grouped into the small beaded cup and saucer. Three are in pale pink and two are in shocking pink, so that they would be in keeping with the same shades that were used for the container. However, a yellow-and-white combination is most attractive, too.

Materials for five lilies, five leaves

Beads: 1 strand for flowers; 3″ of beads in a contrast color; 1 strand green for leaves

Wires: 26-gauge gold spool; 1″ or 2″ 18- or 19-gauge for stem

Lily

Three inches from the open end of the beaded spool wire make 6 continuous loops of beads using 8 beads for loop 1, 14 beads for loop 2, 18 beads for loop 3, 22 beads for loop 4, 22 beads for loop 5, and 26 beads for loop 6. Keep the loops perpendicular, close together, and oval in shape. Allow 4″ of bare wire at the completion of the last loop and cut the wire from the spool. Bring the 6″ of bare wire down the outside of the bottom of the loops and twist it to the beginning wire for ½″. Make 5.

Stamen

Transfer 12 beads of a contrast color to the spool wire, and with a needle or corsage pin, coil the open end of the wire 3 times. Trim off the uncoiled portion and push the 12 beads close to the coil. Allow 3″ of bare spool wire and cut the wire from the spool. Fig. 91. Push the open, unbeaded end of the stamen wire into the center of the lily until the bottom bead of the stamen is at the bottom of the lily—where the smallest loop is—and twist all 3 wires together all the way to the bottom. Make 1 for each lily.

Leaf

Two inches from the open end of the beaded spool wire make a narrow loop of 3″ of green beads and twist both wires together for 1″. Allow 1″ of bare spool wire and cut the wire from the spool. Make 5 (1 for each lily) in green.

Assembly of Cluster

To the top of a short piece of taped 18- or 19-gauge stem wire, tape on the flowers varying the lengths of the stems on each flower. Tape on the leaves, all in the same place, no stems showing on the leaves. Be sure to have the stem wire no longer than the depth of the container to be used, and insert the cluster of flowers and leaves so that none of the master stem shows. Shape the leaves up and curve outward slightly. Bend the heads of the flowers forward.

Fig. 91

2″ long.

CURLY FERN (Shaded and in Miniature)

There is nothing that fills in a small container of miniatures better than the curly fern. It takes so few beads to make them, and they are particularly lovely when done in more than one shade of green.

In order to incorporate more than one shade of beads into the fern, the colors must be pre-strung, and gold wire is the most effective means of doing so. The pattern given here is the standard one, but it may be decreased or increased to suit your individual needs. It can be made with 3 shades of green or 2 shades of green and white, for the outer 3 loops. All of the loops have ten beads.

Put onto a spool of gold wire (26-gauge) 1 strand of the darkest green; then string 40 beads of a medium green; then 30 beads of the lightest green. Four inches from the open end of the spool wire, make a 10-bead loop, twisting both wires together for ¼″. To the left of the 1st loop, and close to the twisted wire, make another 10-bead loop. Directly opposite, and to the right, make another 10-bead loop, and twist both wires together for another ¼″. This will create three 10-bead loops in the lightest color. Continue making pairs of loops with ¼″ of twisted wire in between each pair until you have 2 pairs in the medium shade of green, and 3 pairs in the darker shade. Allow 2 or 3 inches of bare spool wire and cut the wire from the spool. Insert an orange stick, the handle of a small brush, or a pointed pencil into the center of each loop to shape it into a circle. Fig. 92.

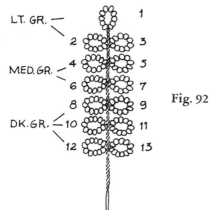

Fig. 92

147

3" long.

CURLY FERN WITH BUD

The fern with bud follows the same principle as the shaded fern inasmuch as the pattern must be prestrung so that the colored beads fall into the right place in the design. All of the loops have 10 beads. Again, this pattern can be changed by lengthening, shortening, and by having more or fewer buds. Use 26-gauge gold wire for this fern also, and transfer 1 strand of green beads to the spool of wire, then string 10 beads in a color, 20 green beads, 10 beads in a color, 20 green beads, 10 beads in a color, and 30 green beads. Four inches from the open end of the spool of wire, make a 10-bead loop and twist the 2 wires together for ¼". To the left of, and close to the twisted wires, make another 10-bead loop. Directly opposite, on the right, make a third 10-bead loop. Without twisting the wires together, make a 10-bead loop in color, directly below the second green loop (on the left), then twist the two wires together for ¼". Make a pair of green loops and directly below the 4th green loop make a 10-bead loop in color. Twist the two wires together for ¼" and make another pair of green loops. Directly below the 6th green loop, make another 10-bead loop in color. Twist the 2 wires together for ¼" and make 3 pairs of green loops (6 in all) and twist together the two wires for ¼" between pairs. Leave 2" of bare spool wire and cut the wire from the spool. Make all of the circles round the same way as the shaded fern, and lift the colored circles to the top of the fern. Fig. 93.

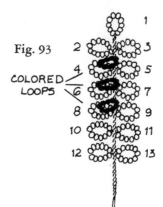

Fig. 93

COLORED
LOOPS

3½″ x 2½″. See also color plate 11.

GERANIUM IN MINIATURE

Some patterns are easy to reduce from full size to miniature, and the geranium is a perfect example. A change in bead size is not necessary.

Materials for one plant with two flower heads

Beads: 6 strands in color for flowers; 6 strands green for leaves
Wires: 26-gauge gold or silver spool; 18-gauge for stems

Flower

Three inches from the crimped end of the beaded spool wire, make a 6-bead loop and give the beaded loop one wraparound with beads, thus creating the 1st petal. Make 3 more, all on the same wire and close together. Fig. 10. Allow 3″ of bare spool wire and cut the wire from the spool. Twist both wires for ½″ to form a stem, and cover each stem with ½-width tape. If gold wire is used, twist both wires together all the way to the end, and do not tape. Make 30, 15 for each head.

Fig. 94

Leaves

Small. BASIC: 5 beads, round top, round bottom, 8 rows. Make 1 for each head.
Work the first 5 rows, and split the basic wire into 2 wires by cutting it open at the bottom of the loop, so that the 2 wires form a narrow *v.* Wrap bare spool wire around the right hand wire 1½ times to reverse the direction of the beading. Bead to the top of the leaf, counterclockwise, wrap bare spool wire around the top basic wire, and bead down the left side, wrapping bare spool wire 1½ times around the wire on the left side of the *v.* Fig. 94. The extra half wrap will again reverse the direction of the beads so that you are in the correct position to bead up to the top of the leaf, working clockwise. This will complete 1 small leaf with 8 rows of beads.

Because there are an even number of rows, the leaf will finish at the top. Allow 3″ of bare spool wire and cut the wire from the spool. Twist the 2 top wires together, bring them down the wrong side of the leaf, and add the 2 bottom wires to them at the narrowest point of the *v,* to form a stem.

Medium. Work the medium leaf in the same way, but give the leaf 12 rows by beading one more time on each side, wrapping one and a half times around the "v" wires. Make 2 for each head.

Large. Work the large leaf in the same way, but give the large leaf 16 rows, working row 13 and 14 on the right and 15 and 16 on the left. Make 1 for each head.

Tape the stems of all leaves with ½-width tape unless gold wire is used.

Assembly of Flower

Around the top of an 18-gauge wire, tape 15 flowers, leaving 1½″ of stem on each flower. Tape down the stem for 1″ and tape on a medium leaf to the left side of the stem. One-inch lower, add a small leaf to the right side of the stem. One-half inch lower, add a medium leaf to the left side, and ½″ lower, add a large leaf to the right side of the stem. Bend the flower head forward, and form the small flowers into a circle. Repeat in the same manner for the second head of flowers.

Use a 4½″ piece of stem wire for one flower head, and a 3¾″ piece for the other.

4″ x 1¾″. See also color plate 13.

HYACINTH MINIATURE

Some miniatures are easily created by reducing the design of its larger counterpart. The hyacinth is a good example. Plant it in a small open salt dish or make the small beaded pot designed for it.

Materials

Beads: 4 strands color; 2 strands green; 48 yellow beads for centers
Wires: 26-gauge gold; 3" piece 18- or 19-gauge for stem

Flower

Allow 2" of bare spool wire at the beginning and end of each flower. Make 4 continuous narrow loops counting 12 beads for each loop. To close the flower, bring the end wire at the base of loop 4 under loop 1, and up between loops 1 and 2. Put 2 yellow beads onto this wire, then cross the wire to the opposite side of the flower and bring it down between loops 3 and 4. Twist the two wires together for 1" to form a stem. Shape the 4 loops up and out to form a small bell. Make 30.

Leaves

BASIC: 1¼", pointed tops, round bottoms, 3 rows. Make 6, in green.
Cut open the basic loop at the bottom of the loop to create 3 wires for the stem. Tape the stem wires with half-width tape.

Assembly of Flower

Using half-width tape, tape a 3" piece of stem wire, and to the top of it tape on 1 flower. ¼" below the first flower, tape on 3 flowers around the stem; ¼" below, tape on 3 or 4 more flowers around the stem. Allow ⅓" of stem on all flowers. Continue adding the remaining flowers around the stem, each row of flowers ¼" below the others. When all flowers have been added, tape to the bottom of the stem. Tape on the 6 leaves, right sides out, 1" below the last row of flowers. Tape to the bottom of the stem, and cut away all flower and leaf wires that extend below the stem wire. Insert the flower stem into the container so that the bottoms of the leaves are even with the top of the container.

1   2   3   4   5

Flower, 1½" x 1¼".
With stem, 3" long.
See also color plate 19.

IRIS (Small)

The small iris is scaled to the small-tipped tulip in the spring arrangement. Color Plate 19 shows them in yellow and white.

Materials for one flower and two leaves

Beads: 1 strand yellow; 1 strand white; 1 strand green
Wires: 28-gauge spool; 18- or 19-gauge for stem

Flower

BASIC: 4 beads, round tops, pointed bottom, 7 rows. Reduce the bottom wires to 2 on all petals. Make 3 petals in white, and 3 petals in yellow.

Leaves

BASIC: 2", pointed tops, round bottoms, 3 rows. Make 2, in green.

Assembly of Flower

Stack the 3 white petals, wrong sides up, bottoms even, and twist the bottom wires together. Trim off top basic wires as usual. Swing the 3 petals into a circle, and cup them upward. Tape the twisted wires and tape the 3 petals to the top of an 18-gauge stem wire. If stems are to be beaded with the green stem beads, hook one end of a 19-gauge wire into the bottom wires of the 3 petals, tape for ½", cut away all petal wires at the base of the tape, attach remaining 3 petals with assembly wire, and proceed as for beaded stems described in Chapter 1. If stems are not to be beaded, add the 3 yellow petals to the base of the mounted white petals with a 12" piece of assembly wire. Attach them right sides up and place one yellow petal between each white petal. Wrap the assembly wire twice, tightly, with each addition, and cut away the excess after the 3rd petal has been added. Tape the exposed petal wires for 1", and cut

152

away the remaining wires. Tape down the stem for 2½" and add a leaf on each side of the stem wire, then continue taping to the bottom of the stem.

Cluster, 3¼" x 2½".
See also color plate 19.

SWEET PEAS (*In Miniature*)

These sweet peas are made in the same pattern as the large ones, but the count has been reduced so that they can be used in bouquets with smaller flowers. The cluster includes 7 flowers and 5 leaves.

Materials

Beads: 5 strands blue; 5 strands white; 4 strands green
Wires: 26-gauge gold spool; 18-gauge for stem

Flower (Make 7)

Unit 1. With bare spool wire, create a basic loop. To the left of the top basic wire, form a narrow, horizontal 6-bead loop. The direction of the loop should be from bottom to top. Wrap bare spool wire around the top basic wire, and form a second narrow, horizontal 6-bead loop on the right, directly opposite the 1st loop. Figs. 50, 51. Secure the spool wire by wrapping it around the bottom basic loop, continue wrapping rows of beads around the 2 horizontal loops until there are 2 on each side, thus giving the small petal 6 rows in all. Allow 4" of bare spool wire at the completion of the 6th row, and cut the wire from the spool. Cut off the top basic wire, leaving only ¼", and flatten it down the wrong side of the petal. Make 1 for each flower in white.

Unit 2. Make this petal the same way, but have 10 beads on each narrow, horizontal loop, and give the petal 8 rows of beads in all. Reduce the bottom wires to 2. Make 1 for each flower in a contrast color.

Assembly of Flower

Onto the extended 4″ of wire at the base of Unit 1, transfer 1½″ of beads in the same color that was used for Unit 2. Form the 1½″ of beads into a narrow loop at the base of the petal, twist the bottom wires together, spiral the loop of beads and press it flat against the right side of the petal. Set the small petal (Unit 1) on top of the large petal (Unit 2), right sides up, bottoms even, and twist the bottom wires all the way down, to form a stem. Fold the petals in half, right sides in, along the center seam of wire, and flare out the outside edges.

Leaves

BASIC: 6 beads, pointed tops, round bottoms, 9 rows. Cut open the basic loop at the bottom of the loop, and twist all 3 wires together all the way down. Make 5, in green.

Assembly of Cluster

To the top of a short piece of 16- or 18-gauge wire (2 or 2¼″) tape all 7 flowers, leaving 2″ of stem on each flower. At the same place, tape on 5 leaves, around the stem, encircling the cluster of 7 flowers. Allow 1″ of stem on each leaf, then tape to the bottom of the stem. Arch the flower stems to form a cascade of blossoms.

Cluster, 2½″ in diameter.
See also color plate 19.

THISTLE (Miniature)

This cluster of small loop flowers is a quick one to make, and you can fill a beaded cup or miniature container with them in no time at all. Group 6 or 7 of them with 5 or 6 miniature palm leaves and a few curly fern for a "thank you" gift.

Materials for one cluster (7 flowers, 6 palm leaves)

Beads: 5 strands for flowers; 3 strands green

1   2   3   4

Flower

Three inches from the crimped end of the beaded spool wire make 14 continuous 1″ loops. Keep the loops narrow. Allow 3″ of bare spool wire and cut the wire from the spool. Twist the 2 wires together to form a stem, swing the first 3 loops to the center, and crush the beaded loops upward to form a blossom. Make 7.

Calyx

Three inches from the crimped end of the beaded spool wire, make 2 continuous 1″ loops. Allow 3″ of bare spool wire and cut the wire from the spool. Make 7, 1 for each flower, in green.

Assembly of Flower

Spread the 2 green loops of the calyx, and set the base of the thistle in the middle of the 2 green loops. Twist both sets of wires together to form a stem. If silver wire has been used, cover the stems of the flowers with ½-width tape. For gold wire, twist the wires tightly to the end and do not tape.

Assembly of Cluster

To the top of a taped piece of 18-gauge wire, tape the flowers, one at a time, allowing 2″ of stem on each flower. Tape on the 6 palm leaves, and a few curly fern. For directions for palm leaf and curly fern see index. Set the cluster deep enough into its container so that the heavy gauge stem wire is completely submerged and not visible.

7″ x 7″. See also color plate 13.

TRELLIS (Beaded)

The beaded trellis has been worked in white opaque beads, and any small climbing flowers can be used with it to create a background for a miniature garden.

Materials

Beads: 1½ bunches of white
Wire: 18-gauge; 30- or 32-gauge lacing
White tape

Cut the 18-gauge wires as follows: 3 wires 7½" long, 2 wires 7¼" long, 2 wires 5¾" long. Cover all wires, individually, with white tape. String the white beads onto a spool of lacing wire and wrap each 18-gauge wire with the white beads. Stack all 7 beaded wires, side by side, so that they are even at the bottom. Combine the 7 wires by wrapping 8 rows of beads around them, 1¼" up from the bottom. Allow 3 or 4 inches of bare spool wire after the 8th row, cut the wire from the spool, wrap the bare wire around the end beaded wire 2 or 3 times to secure, and cut away excess wire close to the beads. Attach the sprigs of miniature bluebells with short pieces of lacing wire and insert 3 curly ferns with buds in the front.

Cluster, 4" x 3½".
See also color plate 13.

TRILLIUM (Miniature)

Trilliums are members of the lily family and their natural colors are all pastels, as well as white. There are 2 clusters of 2 large flowers and 3 small flowers, plus 6 miniature palm leaves, 4 shaded curly fern, and 2 curly fern with buds in the beaded basket.

Materials for one cluster

Beads: ½ bunch for flower petals; 2 strands yellow for centers; 4
  strands medium green; 2 strands light green
Wire: 26-gauge gold

Flower (White)

Each flower has 3 petals, made all-in-one by using the double split basic technique.

Working with a generous basic loop, create a basic of 6 beads, and slide 12 beads into the basic loop before closing it. Make a 5-row petal, pointed top, round bottom, on the 1st 6-bead basic. Divide the 12 beads that are in the basic loop, and put 6 beads on each side. Cut open the basic loop at the bottom of the loop, and make a 5-row petal on each of the other 2 wires that have 6 beads. Figs. 23, 24, 25. You will finish with 1 wire.

Centers

Three inches from the open end of the beaded spool wire, make a 6-bead loop and wrap around it once, with a row of beads, repeat 2 more times, all on the one wire. Allow 3″ of bare wire and cut the wire from the spool. Make 1 for each flower, in yellow.

Small Flower

Make the small flower (in white) with the double split basic also, but give each 6-bead basic petal 3 rows instead of 5.

Centers

Make 3 continuous 6-bead loops, allowing 3″ of bare spool wire at both ends. Make 1 for each small flower, in yellow.

Assembly of Large Flower

Trim off the top basic wires on all of the petals, and place one center in the middle of each flower so that there is a petal under each wraparound loop. Twist the bottom wires together to form a stem. Lift the petals up and out to shape.

Assembly of Small Flower

Trim off top basic wires, and place one center in the middle of each flower. Twist the bottom wires together to form a stem, and lift the petals up and out to shape.

   Palm leaves are described with wild flower, and curly ferns, shaded, and with buds all listed in the index.

Assembly of Cluster

To the top of a short piece of 18-gauge wire, tape 2 large flowers, 3 small flowers, 6 palm leaves, 4 shaded curly fern, and 2 curly fern with buds. The stem wire should be no longer than the depth of the container to be used. For the beaded basket, ¾″ is enough. Trim away all wires that extend below the 18-gauge stem wire, and continue taping to the bottom of the wire. Make a second cluster in the same way. If the beaded basket is going to be used, press a small amount of clay into the center of the basket, cover it with moss, and insert one cluster of flowers on each side, so that the clusters are back to back. Bend the flower heads forward and arrange the leaves between the flowers, and the curly ferns over the edge of the basket.

Cluster, 2½" in diameter.
See also color plates 9, 19.

WILD FLOWER (*Miniature*)

Tiny flower clusters such as these are well scaled to the beaded baskets or small containers such as saccharine boxes or open salt dishes. They have also been used in the "Wedding Cake" arrangement shown in Color Plate 19.

Materials for one cluster (*7 flowers and 5 miniature palm leaves*)

Beads: 2½ strands for flowers; 1 strand in contrast color for centers; 2 strands green for leaves
Wire: 26-gauge gold spool

Flower

Outer unit. Four inches from the crimped end of the beaded spool wire, make 8 continuous loops, counting 12 beads for each loop. Allow 4" of bare spool wire and cut the wire from the spool. Make 7, 1 for each flower.

Inner unit. (Centers). Four inches from the crimped end of the beaded spool wire, make 3 continuous loops, counting 10 beads for each loop. Allow 4" of bare spool wire and cut the wire from the spool. Make 7, 1 for each flower, in a contrasting color.

Assembly of Flower

Place one center unit on top of one outer unit, and twist the wires together to form a stem. This completes one flower. Do the same for the other 6. If silver wire has been used, cover the stems with ½-width tape so that they remain as slim as possible.

Palm Leaf

Crimp the open end of the beaded spool wire and move 1¼″ of beads to the crimped end. Three inches from the opposite end of the 1¼″ of beads, make 4 continuous loops, measuring 1″ of beads for each loop. At the completion of the 4th loop, measure another 1¼″ of beads, push both rows of beads to the base of the loops, and twist the bare wires together to form a stem. Fig. 95. Tape the stems after cutting the wire from the spool. Make 5, in green.

Assembly of Cluster

Tape a short piece of 18-gauge wire, and around the top of it tape on 7 flowers, one at a time, allowing 1½ to 2 inches of stem for each flower. Tape on the leaves, one at a time, in the same place, and at the base of the beaded leaf stem.

IV POTTED PLANTS

Flower 2" in diameter.
See also color plate 15.

BEGONIA

Of the many kinds of begonia, this one seemed to lend itself best to beading. The larger blossoms and trailing buds are perfect for a hanging basket.

Materials for entire arrangement

Beads: 9 bunches for flowers and buds; 3½ bunches medium green; 4 bunches light green
Wires: 26-gauge gold or silver spool; 18-gauge for stem

Flowers

Make 25.

Petals

Large. BASIC: 5 beads, round tops, round bottoms, 9 rows. Make 6 for each flower.
Small. BASIC: 5 beads, round tops, round bottoms, 7 rows. Make 3 for each flower.

Reduce the bottom wires to 2 on all petals and leaves, and work with a generous basic loop.
Bud. BASIC: 5 beads, pointed tops, round bottoms, 7 rows. Make 56, 42 for 14 three-petal buds, 12 for 12 one-petal buds.

Leaves

Small. BASIC: 5 beads, pointed tops, round bottoms, 3 rows. Make 154 (2 for each flower, 4 for each bud), in light green.
Large. BASIC: 4 beads, pointed tops, round bottoms, 11 rows. Make 75, in medium green.

160

Assembly of Flower

Each flower has 6 large petals and 3 small ones. Cup the 3 small petals, wrong sides in, twist the bottom wires together for ½″ to form a stem, and overlap the petals so that they embrace one another. Stack the 6 large petals, one on top of the other, bottoms even, right sides up, and twist the bottom wires together for ½″. Slip the stem of the 3 small petals between any 2 large petals until they are in the center of the 6 petals, then tape the bottom wires together for 1″. Tape 1 small leaf to the left of the stem. Tape down the stem for 1″ and tape on the second small leaf. Allow ½″ of stem on each leaf. Tape an 8- or 9-inch piece of 18-gauge stem wire to the flower stem ½″ below the 2nd small leaf. One inch below, tape on 1 large leaf on the left and ½″ below, add the 2nd large leaf. A half-inch lower add the 3rd large leaf. Allow 1″ of stem on each large leaf. Mount the remaining flowers in the same way.

Assembly of Large Buds

There are 14 buds with 3 petals each. Stack 3 petals, wrong sides up, bottoms even, and twist the bottom wires together to form a stem. Swing the 3 petals into a circle, bow them out at the bottom and bend the tops together until they meet, wrong sides in. Tape the stems. Mount each bud on an 8- or 9-inch piece of 18-gauge stem wire 2″ below the base of the bud, and tape on 4 small leaves with ½″ stems. Place the first leaf 1″ below the base of the bud, the 2nd leaf ½″ lower on the right, the 3rd ½″ lower on the left, and the 4th ½″ lower on the right. Assemble all 14 of the 3-petal buds in the same way.

Assembly of Small Bud

There are 12 small buds with 1 petal each. Spiral one bud petal tightly, wrong side in, and 1″ below the petal, tape on 2 small leaves with 2″ of stem showing on each leaf. Two inches lower, tape on a taped piece of 18-gauge wire and a small leaf. One inch lower, tape on the 4th small leaf, then continue taping to the end of the stem.

If gold wire is used, the petal and leaf stems need not be taped. Add the leaves to the flower and bud wires by twisting them together, then tape on the 18-gauge stem wires 2 or 2½″ below the base of the flowers and buds.

14½" x 6".
See also color plate 16.

CROWN IMPERIAL (Fritillaria imperialis)

This spectacular plant is one of the spring-blooming bulbs. The large clusters of flowers that form the crest at the top of the stem grow not only in the brilliant salmon, as shown in Color Plate 16, but also in yellow, crimson, brown, pale green and purple.

Materials for one plant (7 flowers, 5 buds)

Beads: 2 bunches color for flowers and buds; 2 bunches green for leaves; 2 strands yellow for stamens

Wires: four 16-gauge for stem; 26- or 28-gauge spool

Petals

Make 5 petals for each flower using single split basic technique. Working with a generous basic loop, create a basic with 8 beads on the top basic wire, and put 9 beads into the basic loop. Fig. 96. Give the top basic beads 2 rows of beads on each side (5 rows in all, including the basic), round top and round bottom. At the completion of the 5th row of beads, wrap spool wire 1½ times so that it is to the right of the 5 rows of beads. Transfer the 9 beads that are in the basic loop to one side of the loop. Cut open the basic loop on the opposite side and crimp the open end of the wire. Bead down the right side of the 9 beads, wrap spool wire once around the bare wire at the base of the 9 beads, keeping the 9 beads close to the base of the top unit of 5 rows. Give the entire petal one row of beads on both sides, wrapping around the top basic wire as you work, A in Fig. 97 and the bottom basic wire as well, B in Fig. 97. Allow 5" of bare wire and cut it from the spool. Trim off the top basic wire as usual.

Bud

There are three 2-petal buds and two 3-petal buds in the arrangement.

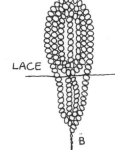

Fig. 96

CUT —

Fig. 97

— CUT

A

LACE

B

162

Therefore make 12 extra flower petals for the buds, same color as flower petals.

Stamen

Make an 8-bead loop of beads and give the loop 3 half twists to close the wires at the base of the loop. Push 16 beads close to the base of the loop. At the opposite end of the 16 beads create a basic loop of wire. Push 16 more beads close to the basic loop and at the top of these 16 beads, make another 8-bead loop. Fig. 53. Trim off wires *A* and *B* close to the base of the beaded loops. Make 7, 1 for each flower, in yellow.

Leaves in Green

All have pointed tops and round bottoms
Size A. BASIC: 2″, 5 rows. Make 8 for the top and 4 for the bottom (12 in all).
Size B. BASIC: 2½″, 5 rows. Make 6 for the top and 10 for the bottom (16 in all).
Size C. BASIC: 3″, 5 rows. Make 4 for the top only.
Size D. BASIC: 3½″, 7 rows. Make 5 for the bottom.
Tape the stems of all the leaves.

Assembly of Flower and Buds

For each flower, lace 5 petals together, right sides up, at the base of the 7-row unit. Fig. 97. Fold the 5 petals in half, wrong sides in, and close the flower by twisting together the 2 lacing wires. Cut away all but ¼″ of the twisted lacing wires and tuck ¼″ of wire to the inside of the flower. Insert a stamen in the center of the flower and twist together the petal and stamen wires to form a stem. Tape the stem. Cup the top of the petals out then in to form a bell.

For each 2-petal bud, lace together 2 petals, and for each 3-petal bud, lace together 3 petals. Close them the same way as for the flower, twist the bottom wires together to form a stem and tape the stems.

Assembly of Plant

Individually tape four 16-gauge wires, 10″ long, then tape them together, side by side, to form a sturdy stem. Around the top of the stem, tape on 4 of the smallest leaves (size *A*), right sides up, with no stem showing on the leaves. Tape down the stem for ¼″

and add 4 more of the smallest leaves, right sides up no stem showing, then 6 of size *B* in the same way. Tape down the stem for another ¼″ and tape on the buds. Add them around the stem and allow 1¼″ of stem on each bud. Alternate the buds, one large, one small, one large, etc. Tape down the stem for ¼″ and around the stem add the 4 leaves from size *C*. Tape down the stem for ¼″ and around the stem tape on the 7 flowers, leaving 2″ stems on all of them so that they will hang down like bells.

Two and a half inches up from the bottom of the stem wire, tape on the remaining leaves starting with the smaller ones, 10 of the next size and finally, the 5 largest ones. Curve all of the leaves up and out, and arrange the 5 largest ones across the front of the container.

Flowers, 4¼″ x 4″.
Stalk with leaves, 11″ high.
See also color plate 16.

EASTER LILY (*Lilium longiflorum*)

Long associated with the Easter holidays and a great favorite of florists in the early spring is the elegant, waxen Easter Lily, its long stems lushly trimmed with pointed leaves. Not only is the potted plant attractive, but the blossoms may be treated as cut flowers for bouquets.

Materials for one plant

Beads: 2 bunches white alabaster, opaline or pearl; 2 bunches green; 1 strand yellow
Wires: 26-gauge spool; 14- or 16-gauge for stem

Flower Petals

BASIC: 2″, pointed tops, pointed bottoms, 11 rows.
Reduce the bottom wires to 2, by cutting open the basic loop at the base of the petals.

For each flower, lace 6 petals together, right sides up, so that the lacing will not show on the inside of the flowers. Fold the laced petals in half to join the lacing wires and close the flower. Twist the lacing wires together for ½", cut away all but ¼" of the twisted wires, and tuck the twisted wires between 2 petals. Make 6 for each flower.

Stamens

Four inches from the open end of the spool wire, make a narrow loop with 1" of yellow beads, bead up the front and down the back of the loop, wrap bare spool wire twice, tightly, at the base of the loop, and cut off the spool wire very close to the base of the loop. Onto the remaining wire, put 2¼" of green beads, and set aside. Make 2 more stamens in the same way, group the 3 stamens together, and twist their 3 bare wires together to form a stem. Keep the green beads tight, between the yellow loop and the bottom twisted wires. Tape the stem. Make 3 for each flower, in yellow with green stems.

Flower Calyx

Create a basic with 10 beads for the basic row, and 10 beads on row 2. Wrap bare spool wire twice, tightly, at the finish of the 2nd row. Insert a round pencil between the 2 rows of beads to create a circle. Around this circle of beads, wrap beaded wire, securing each row by wrapping bare spool wire, as usual, around the top and bottom basic wires until 15 rows of beads have been completed, 7 rows on each side of the circle, but use 14 beads for rows 3 and 4, 16 beads for rows 5 and 6, 18 beads for rows 7 and 8, 20 beads for rows 9 and 10, and 22 beads for rows 11, 12, 13, and 14. Cut open the basic loop at the bottom of the loop. Bring both sets of wires (2 from each side) into the center and out through the small circle at the bottom. Make 1 for each flower, in green.

Leaves

BASIC: 2¾", pointed tops, round bottoms, 7 rows. Lace each leaf once, through the middle, right sides up, and tape the stems. Make 18, (10 for the tallest lily and 8 for the shortest one) in green.

Assembly of Flower

To the top of a taped stem wire, cut to desired length, tape a cluster of 3 stamens. Insert the opposite end of the stem wire into the flower petals until the bottom beading of the stamens reaches the

1   2   3   4   5

bottom of the petals. Tape the petal wires to the stem wire for 1½″, and cut petal wires away. Insert the open end of the stem wire into the center of the green calyx. Push the calyx close to the base of the flower, cover the calyx wires with tape to secure, tape down the stem for 1½″ and add the first pair of leaves, right sides up, and opposite one anotner. Add the remaining leaves with tape, spacing them 1½″ apart, and opposite one another. Bend the head of the flower forward. Repeat in the same manner for the 2nd flower.

Bud

Stack the two petals, one green and one white, wrong sides in, bottoms even, twist the bottom wires together and tape them. Spiral the 2 petals tightly, so that the green one wraps around the white one, then mount the bud to the top of a taped 16-gauge stem wire. Add 2 or 4 more leaves to the stem, if you wish, and tape the bud to the stem of either flower, joining the stem wires with tape below the leaves. Make 1 petal in white, and repeat in green.

Flower, 6″ x 5″.
Plant, 20″ x 8½″.
See also color plate 16.

GIANT IRIS

This stately flower towers over everything else in the garden, and each blossom measures 6″ high and 5″ wide. The color choice is almost limitless, as they grow in solid white, and yellow, shaded blues, lavenders, and maroon red. The Iris shown in Color Plate 16 is made of white alabaster and transparent French lavender, and each petal is shaded, featuring more white in the 3 upper petals, and more lavender in the 3 down petals, with a touch of pale yellow for the stamen and 3 short beards. The materials listed below are for a solid-color flower. If you shade the petals, use half that amount in 2 colors.

Materials for one flower in solid color

Beads: 1¾ bunches for petals; 1½ strands yellow; 1½ bunches green
Wires: 26-gauge spool; 18- or 19-gauge for bracing petals; 12- or 14-gauge for stem

Unit 1. BASIC: 1", round tops, pointed bottoms, 25 rows. Large petals; make 6. When the 25th row has been completed, leave 4" of bare spool wire and cut the wire from the spool. Reduce the bottom wires to 2 by cutting open the basic loop on one side at the base of the petal. Leave 1½" of top basic wire on all petals, and tape it. Use a color that blends well with the beads. Tape comes in a wide range of colors. Tape a 10" piece of 18- or 19-gauge stem wire for each petal. Tape 1 piece to the top basic wire of each petal and bring the stem wire down the wrong side of the petal to reinforce it. Fig. ...... Tape the bottom wires together, and lace each petal, individually, through the middle, including the reinforcing wire in the lacing. Reinforce and lace each petal.

Unit 2. BASIC: 1", round tops, round bottoms, 7 rows. Make 3 for each flower. Reduce the bottom wires to 2, the same as for the larger ones. Leave 2" of bare spool wire and cut the wire from the spool. Trim off the top basic wires as always, and bend down the wrong side of the petals.

Unit 3. Stamen. Make 1 in a contrast color. Make a narrow loop of beads, measuring 3" of beads for the loop. Give the loop a 4-row crossover by beading up the front and down the back of the narrow loop. It will measure 1½" when completed. Twist together and tape the bottom wires and spiral the loop by giving the loop of beads 2 full twists.

Unit 4. Beard. Make 3 in a contrast color. Each of the petals that bend downward has a short beard attached to it. Measure 5" of beads, close it into a narrow loop, twist the bottom wires together, and spiral the loop by giving it 2 full twists. Set one beard on the right side of each of the down petals, bottoms even, and twist the wires of the beard around the petal wires. Secure the top of the beard to the petal with a small piece of lacing wire, twist the lacing wire ends together on the wrong side of the petal, cut away the excess and flatten against the wrong side of the petal.

Assembly of Flower

Tape a piece of 12- or 14-gauge wire that has been cut to the desired length. (Plate 16 used 15″ pieces.) Tape the stem wire to the base of the stamen. Attach a 25″ piece of 30- or 32-gauge lacing wire to the base of the stamen, wrapping it around the stem wire 3 or 4 times to secure. With the lacing wire, add the 3 up petals, one at a time, wrong sides facing in, wrapping the lacing wire around the stem wire 3 or 4 times with each addition. Add one small petal (Unit 2) between each up petal, wrong sides in, then add the 3 down petals, one at a time, right sides up, directly underneath each small petal. Be sure to wrap the lacing wire tightly. When all petals have been added, wrap lacing wire down the stem a few extra times, cut away the excess, and cover the petal wires and the stem wire with tape. Let the petal stem wires hang straight down the master stem. Don't wrap them around it. If they are too long, trim off 2 or 3 inches before taping over them. Wrap the stem with green beads that have been strung on lacing wire, and wrap for about 11½″.

Leaves

BASIC: 7½″, pointed top, round bottom, 11 rows.

If green stem beads are available, use them for the 7½″ basic on 19-gauge wire. (See General Instructions for Beaded Stems.) If they are not, make the leaf in the normal way and reinforce down the back of each leaf the same way you did the petals, but use green tape on the 18- or 19-gauge wire.

Whichever method is used, lace the leaves, individually, in 3 places, and tape them to the flower stem, at the base of the beading on the stem. Make 2 or 3, in green.

Bud

BASIC: 1″, round top, pointed bottom, 13 rows.

Trim off the top basic wires on both, and reduce to 2 the bottom wires. Stack the two petals, one on top of the other, bottoms even, twist the bottom wires together, and tape the stem wires. Coil the two petals so that the green one wraps around the colored one. Tape the top of a taped 16-gauge stem wire to the base of the coiled bud petals, wrap the stem with green beads for 5 or 6 inches and tape it to the flower stem at the base of the beading. Make one in green and one in the color of the petal.

```
L____,____|____1____,____2____,____3____,____4____,____|
           1         2         3         4
```

Shading the Petals

The top petals are started in white. Work the basic of 1″ and 9 rows in white. Allow 2 yards of bare spool wire and cut the wire from the spool. Onto the 2 yards of wire, put 10 beads in a contrast color for the bottom of the 10th row, enough white beads for the remainder of the 10th row and the top part of the 11th row, then 10 beads in the contrast color for the bottom of the 11th row. For each succeeding even-numbered row, add 4 more beads in the contrast color and decrease by 4 beads of the original color on each odd-numbered row.

The 3 down petals are reversed, starting with the contrast color. The same pattern is followed for the shading.

Flower heads, 5¼″ in diameter.
See also color plate 16.

HYDRANGEA

We are accustomed to seeing hydrangeas with their huge rounded heads in shades of blues, but there are many other colors including pinks, lavenders and white. Hydrangeas look best surrounded by their own massive foliage, or as a focal point in a simple arrangement.

Materials for a two-headed plant

Beads: 2 bunches dark blue; 8 strands pale blue; 2 strands yellow; 5 bunches green
Wires: 26-gauge spool; 14- or 16-gauge for stem

Flower

String 1 strand light blue beads, and crimp the open end of the wire. Eight inches from the crimped end of the wire, make 4 continuous 10-bead loops. Leave ¼″ of bare wire between each loop, and at the completion of the 4th loop allow 12″ of bare spool wire, then cut the wire from the spool. Feed onto the 12″ of bare wire about 9″ of the darker blue beads. Wrap once around the 4th loop with a row of beads, wrap twice around the 3rd loop with beads, once around the 2nd loop, and twice around the 1st loop. Fig. 98. Both end wires will be at the base of the first loop. Bring the longest wire under the 4th loop and up between the 4th and 5th loops to close the flower. Onto this same wire, transfer 6 yellow beads. Push them close to the base of the blue petals, and form them into a small loop by folding the beads in half, and twisting the loop of beads twice, tightly, to cross the wires at its base. Press the loop flat and in the center of the flower, and bring the bare wire down between petals 1 and 2. Wrap this wire 4 or 5 times around the other wire, close to the base of the flower, and cut it off, close to the one remaining wire. Onto the remaining wire, transfer 3″ of medium stem beads, or the regular green beads, and cover the remaining bare wire below the beads with tape. Fig. 99. Make 35 for each head.

Assembly of Flower

When all 35 flowers for 1 head are completed, tape two 10″ 16-gauge wires, individually, and then together, side by side, for extra support. To the top of the stem wires, tape on all flowers, at the base of the beading, one at a time, and all in the same place, around the top of the wire.

Mount the other 35 flowers for the second head to the top of two 7½″ pieces of 16-gauge wires in the same way.

Leaves

Large. BASIC: 7 beads, pointed tops, round bottoms, 25 rows. Make 15, in green.
Small. BASIC: 7 beads, pointed tops, round bottoms, 19 rows. Make 15.

Assembly of Leaves

Combine 3 small leaves by stacking them, one on top of the other, right sides up, bottoms even, then twist the bottom wires together for 1″. Swing the leaves into a circle, cup them in the center, deeply with your thumb, then bend back the tips of the leaves.

Combine 3 large leaves in the same way, and join the two sets of leaves by sliding the stem wires of the 3 small leaves between 2

Fig. 98

of the larger leaves. Twist both sets of stem wires together and tape them. Make 5 clusters.

Mount each leaf cluster to the top of a taped piece of 16-gauge wire. Cut 2 wires 5″ long, 2 wires 4″ long, and 1 wire 3″ long. One inch below the base of the highest flower stem, and on the right, tape one 5″ cluster of leaves, and allow 3½″ of stem on the leaf cluster so that the leaves are higher than the flower head. Two and a half inches below the flower head, and on the left, tape on the other 5″ leaf cluster, allowing 2″ of stem on the leaf cluster. Three and one-half inches below the base of the 2nd flower head, and to the left, tape on one 4″ leaf cluster, allowing 1″ of stem on the leaf cluster. One inch lower, and on the right, add the other 4″ cluster of leaves. One-half inch lower, and in the front, add the last leaf cluster, and allow ½″ of stem. Bend the heads of the flowers forward and pot them in a container that measures approximately 4″ x 4½″.

Fig. 99

26″ x 14″.
See also color plate 23.

MING TREE

This tree has been built on a branch of dried manzanita. To it has been added needlelike tufts of green beads made like the Spider Chrysanthemum units, and in various lengths.

Materials

Beads: 4 bunches green
Wire: 26- or 28-gauge spool
Tape: Brown or twig
Darning needle or corsage pin

All tufts are made in the same way, but the measurements change.

1   2   3   4   5

Unit 1. Wrap the open end of the beaded spool wire 3 times around the pointed end of a needle, and push ¾" of beads to the base of the coiled wire. At the base of the beads, make a basic loop with bare wire. Push ¾" of beads to the basic loop, and at the opposite end of the second ¾" of beads wrap bare wire around the pointed end of the needle 6 times. Fig. 67. Keep the coils close together. Cut open the basic loop at the bottom of the loop, cut away any uncoiled wire at the top of the first coil, and cut in the middle of the 6 coils. This will leave the open end of the spool wire already coiled for the making of the next pair. Make 32 pairs, and divide them into 8 groupings of 4 pairs each by taping the bottom wires of 4 pairs together 8 times.

Unit 2. Unit 2 is made the same as Unit 1, but the amount of beads between each coil increases to 1" instead of ¾". Make 60 pairs for 10 groupings of 6 pairs.

Unit 3 is made the same way, but the amount of beads between each coil increases to 1¼", and you need 88 pairs for 11 groupings of 8 pairs each.

Unit 4 is made the same way, but the amount of beads between each coil increases to 1½" and you need 90 pairs for 9 groupings of 10 pairs each.

Tape the units to the tree branches, placing most of the smaller tufts at the outer tips of the branches, then add the medium and larger sizes lower down.

8" x 9½".
See also color plates 13, 16.

STRAWBERRY PATCH

The strawberries are made like the beehive centers of anemones, and the wild tansy flower.

Materials for one plant

Beads: 9 strands red; 4 strands pale green; 3 strands white; 2 strands yellow; 9 strands medium green; 2½ bunches dark green

Wires: 28-gauge spool; 18-gauge for stem

Red Strawberries

Work with a generous basic loop and top wire. Create a 2-bead basic, follow the count of beads for each row, and make each count of beads fit between the wires.

For row 2, use 4 beads; for row 3, 5 beads; for row 4, 6 beads; for row 5, 7 beads; for row 6, 8 beads; for row 7, 9 beads; for row 8, 10 beads; for row 9, 11 beads; for row 10, 12 beads; for row 11, 13 beads; for row 12, 14 beads; for row 13, 15 beads; for row 14, 16 beads; for row 15, 16 beads; for row 16, 16 beads; for row 17, 17 beads; for row 18, 17 beads; for row 19, 16 beads; for row 20, 16 beads; for row 21, 15 beads; for row 22, 15 beads; for row 23, 14 beads; and for row 24, 14 beads. The berry will finish at the single wire. Cut open the basic loop at the bottom of the loop, and bring both sets of wires to the center of the opening at the top of the berry. Twist the two sets of wires together to form a stem. Make 10.

Calyx for Red Berry

Make 5 continuous 3-row crossover loops, measuring 1½″ of beads for the initial loop. Fig. 12. Make 10, in medium green.

Small Green Berry

Follow the pattern for the red berry, but work only through the 12th row, bring both sets of wires together at the top of each berry and twist them together to form a stem. Make 12, in light green.

Small Green-and-White Berry

Follow the pattern for the small green berry, working the first 7 rows in light green. Allow 10″ of bare wire, cut the wire from the spool, and feed on enough white beads to work the next 5 rows. (about 3″). Make 5, in light green and white.

Calyx for Small Berry

Make 5 continuous loops, measuring 1″ of beads for each loop. Make 17, in medium green.

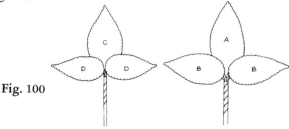

Fig. 100

Assembly of Berries

To the top of each large red berry add a large calyx, wrong side in, and twist both calyx and berry wires together to form a stem. Cover the wires with ½-width tape.

To the top of each small berry add a small calyx, and twist both sets of wires together to form a stem. Keep the calyx loops narrow, and curl their tips backwards, away from the berry and toward the stem.

Flower

The flower has 6 petals, made all in one. Each petal has an 8-bead loop with one wraparound. Fig. 10. Allow 2″ of bare spool wire at both ends, combine them in the center of the wrong side of the petals and twist together to form a stem. Make 9, in white.

Flower Stamen

Make one 8-bead loop and set it flat, and in the center of the flower. Twist the stamen wires to the flower wires and cover with ½-width tape. Make 9, in yellow.

Leaves

The leaves are made in 4 sizes in dark green, and are grouped in clusters of threes. All leaves have pointed tops and round bottoms.
Size A. BASIC: 4 beads, 15 rows; make 8.
Size B. BASIC: 4 beads, 13 rows; make 16.
Size C. BASIC: 8 beads, 9 rows; make 6.
Size D. BASIC: 8 beads, 7 rows; make 12.

Cover the stems of all leaves with tape, group them into clusters of threes and tape the stems together, close to the base of the leaves. Tape 2 size *B* leaves to each size *A* leaf, and tape 2 size *D* leaves to each size *C* leaf. This will make 8 groupings of 1 *A* and 2 *B's,* and 6 groupings of 1 *C* and 2 *D's.* Fig. 100.

Mount each cluster of three leaves to a short piece of taped 18-gauge stem wire. Mount each berry and each flower to a taped piece of 18-gauge stem wire. Vary the lengths of the stems on all berries and flowers between 5½″ and 1½″ inches. Set the leaf groupings lower; 4 to 1 inches.

The strawberry patch is arranged on an oval piece of heavy cardboard, cut free-form, measuring approximately 8″ by 6″. The cardboard is covered with clay and moss. The clay is mounded to a height of 1½″ to the left of center, and sloped downward, close to the edge of the cardboard. Nearly all of the flowers and berries are planted into the deepest part of the clay mound, and the leaf groupings are around the outer edge.

There are 7 individual strawberries, all red, in the small basket shown in Color Plate 13. No stem wire has been added, but the calyx and berry wires have been taped together and coiled.

12½″ x 3¼″.

TOPIARY (*Double Ball*)

The double-balled topiary is made in the same way as the large single ball, except that two 2½″ Styrofoam balls were used. It is described fully under "Topiary, Single Ball."

Materials

Beads: 4 bunches blue; ½ bunch yellow; 1 bunch green
Wires: four 12″ pieces 16-gauge for stem; 26-gauge spool

There are 32 flowers and 10 leaves on each ball. Cover each ball with flowers and leaves. Starting at the top of the top ball with 1 flower, 6 flowers below and around it, 10 flowers below and around the 6 until the ball is completely covered. Insert the leaves, here and there, between the flowers, to fill any bare areas. Trim the lower ball in the same way, but eliminate the top flower. This space will be left bare for the stem wires.

Tape individually, then together, side by side, four 16-gauge wires 12″ long. Push these combined wires all the way into the bottom of the top ball. Starting at the base of the top ball, wrap the stem wires with green beads that have been strung on lacing wire. Wrap for 2″. At the completion of the 2″, wrap bare lacing wire around the stem 3 or 4 times to secure, then cut away the excess. Push the second ball from the bottom of the stem wires to the base of the beaded stem. Attach beaded lacing wire to the stem wires directly under the lower ball, and wrap the stem with beads for 2½ or 3 inches, depending on the depth of the container that is to be used. Make a few extra leaves and flowers, mount them to a short piece of stem wire and add them to the container.

12″ x 4″.

TOPIARY (Single Ball)

There are an infinite number of different ways to create the topiary. Styrofoam shapes are available in cones as well as balls from 1 to 4 inches in diameter. The one shown here uses a white, 3″ ball that was wrapped with yellow floral tape, and it is solidly covered with 60 small, yellow flowers and 40 small leaves. The "trunk" is a 10″ piece of ¼″ dowelling, 2″ of which has been inserted and glued into the base of the ball. When all flowers and leaves were added to the ball, the dowel was taped and then wrapped in green beads that had been strung on 32-gauge assembly wire.

Materials

Beads: 4 bunches beads for flowers; ½ bunch in contrast color for centers; ½ bunch green
Wire: 26-gauge spool

Flower

Crimp the open end of the beaded spool of wire, and 2″ from the crimped end of the wire make a 10-bead loop. Wrap twice around the 10-bead loop with rows of beads, secure each wraparound by wrapping bare spool wire around the base of the petal that is being created. Leave ¼″ of bare wire between the completed petal and the start of a new one. This space will be filled when the next 2 wraparounds are completed. Make another 10-bead loop, and give 2 wraparounds of beads. Continue for 3 more petals, allow 2″ of bare spool wire, and cut the wire from the spool. Fig. 10. Make at least 60.

Flower Centers

One inch from the crimped end of the beaded spool wire, make 4 continuous 10-bead loops. Twist the end wires together to form a stem, allow 1″ of bare spool wire, and cut the wire from the spool. Make 1 for each flower, as in fig. 9, but with only 4 loops.

Leaf

One inch from the crimped end of the beaded spool wire, make a narrow loop of 15 beads. Wrap around the outer edge of the beaded loop with beaded wire, twist the two bottom wires together very tightly to form a stem, and cut the wire from the spool. Reduce the leaf wires to 1″. Make 40, in green.

Assembly of Flowers

Set one center into each of the flowers, and twist both sets of wires together very tightly. Cut away all but ½″ of the wires. If the stem wires of the flowers and leaves are twisted very tightly, they will push into the styrofoam ball very easily.

Assembly of Topiary

Starting at the top of the ball, insert the stem of 1 flower. Around the first flower, insert the stems of 5 flowers, one at a time, so that the petals of the flowers merely touch one another, not overlap. Continue adding flowers around and down the ball until all have been added. In between the flowers, add the leaves.

Insert the dowel into the bottom of the ball for 2″. Tape the remaining portion of the dowel. Starting at the base of the ball, attach assembly wire that has been strung with green beads. Wrap the green beads around the dowel to within 3″ of the bottom. Keep the rows of beads close together. At the base of the beading, wrap several times with bare wire, to secure, and cut the wire from the spool. Insert the topiary into a container of your choice. Trim the base of the topiary with a few extra flowers and leaves if you desire.

V *HOLIDAY ORNAMENTS*

1½″ high, 2″ wide at base.
See also color plate 22.

BEADED TREE STAND (For Small Christmas Tree)

It takes about 4 strands of green beads to make the stand. Make the frame of 24-gauge wire, 6 pieces cut 4″ long, and combine them the same as for all the beaded containers, by stacking the wires evenly, and twisting one end of them for ¾″. With the twisted ends up, spread the 6 wires like 6 legs. Fig. 101. Attach the open end of the beaded wire (32-gauge) at the base of the twisted wires. Starting at the base of 1 leg, use 2 beads for the first row, 3 beads for the second row, and 4 beads for the third row, then keeping the legs spread and evenly spaced, use just enough beads to fill the spaces between each leg until 17 rows have been completed. Wrap bare spool wire 2 or 3 times around the last leg, and cut away the spool wire. Allow ¼″ of frame wire beyond the beading on each leg, and cut away the excess. Bend the remaining ¼″ of frame wire flat against the inside of the stand. Insert the ¾″ of twisted frame wires into the center of the bottom of the tree.

Fig. 101

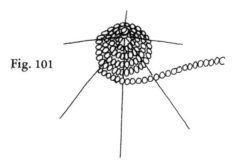

CANDY CANES

No Christmas tree is ever complete without candy canes for the small guests. These are not edible, to be sure, but they are simple to make and very effective.

Materials for one

Beads: 22″ white opaque; 11″ red opaque
Wire: 26-gauge spool

Cane

Make, individually, 2 narrow loops of white beads, measuring 11″ of beads for each loop. Make the same thing in red, using the same measurements. Stack all three loops, one on top of the other, bottoms even, and twist the bottom wires together. Cut away all but ¼″ of the twisted wires, bend the ¼″ of twisted wires upward and tuck them in between the rows of beads. Spiral the loops of beads so that 4 rows of white alternate with 2 rows of red. Bend down the top to resemble a cane.

CHRISTMAS TREE LIGHT REFLECTORS

These reflectors are a series of continuous loops. The size described here is for the very tiny bulbs, and it may be necessary for you to adjust the pattern to fit the size bulb you will be using. The number of loops used determine the diameter of the circle when the loops are closed, so, of course, more loops, larger circle.

Materials for one reflector

Beads: 1½ strands silver, gold, red or green silver-lined bugles
Wire: 26- or 28-gauge spool

Reflector

Three inches from the open end of the beaded spool wire, make 18 continuous loops, measuring 1½" of beads for each loop. Allow 3" of bare spool wire and cut the wire from the spool. Bring the end wire under loop 1 and up between loops 1 and 2 so that loop 18 and 1 are close together, thus forming the loops into a circle. Bring the wire across the base of loop 2 and down between loops 2 and 3, up between loops 3 and 4, and down between loops 4 and 5. Cut away the excess wire close to the base of the loops. With the remaining piece of wire, back weave in the opposite direction by bringing the wire under loop 18, up between loops 18 and 17, etc. until you have gone halfway around the circle of loops. Cut away the wire close to the beads. To use these reflectors on strung Christmas tree lights, remove the bulbs, set on the reflectors, and replace the bulbs.

(Large) 3¼" in diameter.
(Small) 2" in diameter.
See also color plate 22.

CHRISTMAS TREE SNOWFLAKES

There are many combinations that are possible in the snow-flake pattern. Use them in several sizes for large Christmas tree decorations, for festive trim across an archway, to add a bit of extra glamour to a gift package, or a touch of whimsey to draperies.

Patterns 1 and 2 are made with ¼" bugle beads in either silver or gold. They are continuous petals made all on one wire. Pattern 1 has alternating petals, one short, one long, etc., until there are 12 in all, 6 of each size. It takes 2 strands of beads for the large pattern and 1 strand for Pattern 2.

| 1 | 2 | 3 | 4 |

Pattern 1

Transfer 2 strands of ¼″ silver-lined bugle beads to a spool of either 26- or 28-gauge wire, and crimp the open end. Move 8 beads to the crimped end of the wire. Two inches from the crimped end, make a 4-bead loop, twisting the loop of beads to cross the wires at the base of the loop. Wrap a row of beads around the outer rim of the 4-bead loop, wrap bare spool wire around the base of the double loop to secure the wraparound. Fig. 102. Push the original 8 beads to the base of the double loop, push 8 more beads from the wire to the base of the double loop, creating 2 parallel rows of 8 beads each. Wrap bare spool wire around the wire at the base of the 2 rows of beads, thus making the first petal. Push 4 beads to the base of the first petal and make a 4-bead loop at the top of the 4 beads. Wrap beads around the 4-bead loop, and bead down to the bottom of the row of 4 beads with 4 beads. Cross bare spool wire around the base of the second petal to secure. Push 8 beads to the base of the second petal, and make a 4-bead loop at the top. Wrap around, once with beads, and bead down to the bottom of the 8 beads using 8 beads. Secure by wrapping bare spool wire around the base of the third petal. Continue until there are 6 small petals alternating with 6 large petals. When the 12th petal has been made, allow 5″ of bare spool wire and cut the wire from the spool. Twist the two wires together to bring the petals into a circle, and use the remaining wires for hanging the snowflake.

Pattern 2

Pattern 2 is made the same way except for a change of count. There are only 8 petals and all of them are the same size; 4 beads for the loop with one wraparound, and a double row of 4 beads at the base of each loop instead of 8 beads. Make the petals continuously, the same as for Pattern 1. Fig. 103.

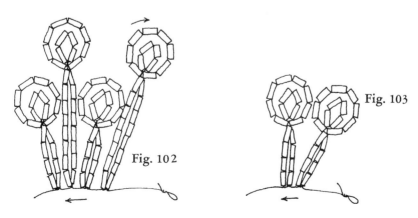

Fig. 102

Fig. 103

Small tree, 8¼'' high, 3¼'' wide at base.
See also color plate 22.

CHRISTMAS TREE (Small)

This little tree uses a green 6'' styrofoam cone as its base, and is trimmed with beaded leaves in 4 sizes. It takes approximately 3 bunches of green beads and is trimmed with a few strands of gold bugle beads that are draped in swags that are held in place with gold-headed pins and small clusters of large red beads that resemble holly berries. There are many other ways to decorate it, so let your imagination have fun. If it is difficult to find a green cone for the base, spray a white one with a shade of green paint that blends best with the green beads you will be using, or cover it with green tape. Twenty-six-gauge spool wire is best for the leaves.

Leaves

All leaves have a 6-bead basic and all have pointed tops and round bottoms.

Unit A. Make 26 with 11 rows.
Unit B. Make 21 with 9 rows.
Unit C. Make 26 with 7 rows.
Unit D. Make 19 with 5 rows.

Cut open the basic loop at the bottom of the loop on all leaves. Twist the 3 wires together, tightly, for 1'' and cut away all but ½''. With a pencil, mark off lines and dots on the cone as shown in Fig. 104. Starting at the bottom line, insert one Unit *A* leaf stem into each dot. Be sure to push the stem of the leaf all the way into the Styrofoam cone. It takes about 14 leaves for the first row. Bend each leaf down and press them flat against the cone. Into the dots on row 2, insert 12 more leaves from Unit *A* in the same way and flatten them against the cone. Into the dots on row 3, insert 11 leaves of Unit *B*. Into the dots on row 4, insert 10 leaves of Unit *B*. Into the dots on row 5, insert 10 leaves of Unit *C*. Into the dots on row 6, insert 9 leaves of Unit *C*. Into the dots on row 7, insert 7 leaves of Unit *C*. Into the dots on row 8, insert 7 leaves of Unit

Fig. 104

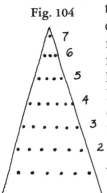

1¼'' BETWEEN
ROWS

D. Into the dots on row 9, insert 6 leaves of Unit *D.* With the remaining 6 small leaves of Unit *D,* make two sets of 3 leaves each as follows: stack 3 leaves, one on top of the other, right sides up, bottoms even, and twist the stem wires together, tightly. Cut off all but 2/3″ of the wires. Repeat with the remaining 3 leaves. Combine both sets of leaves by stacking them, face to face (right sides in), and taping the stems together. Insert the taped wires into the top of the tree and bend the leaves down to cover the top of the cone.

Into the center of the bottom of the cone, insert a 3″ piece of ¼″ wooden dowel to serve as a trunk. Tape the dowel, wrap it with green beads that have been strung on a 30- or 32-gauge spool wire, and insert the beaded trunk into a small container of your choice.

If you prefer the beaded tree stand as shown in the photograph, insert the top twisted wires of the frame into the center of the bottom of the Styrofoam cone, and the tree is ready to stand on its own.

Large tree, 11½″ high, 4″ wide at base.
See also color plate 22.

CHRISTMAS TREE (*Large*)

This tree is built on a 9″ styrofoam cone. The cones are usually available in white or pale green. This one was wrapped with green floral tape. All of the leaves are the same size, and the swags of gold bugle beads are held in place with gold-headed corsage pins that have been cut to a 1″ length. Let your creative abilities have fun with the trimming, by using bits and pieces from discarded costume jewelry, for example.

Materials

Beads: 3 bunches medium or dark green transparent; 4 strands bugle for swags
Wire: 26-gauge spool

Leaves—Make 61

BASIC: 8 beads, pointed tops, round bottoms, 13 rows.

Allow 2″ of bare spool wire at the completion of each leaf, and cut the wire from the spool. Cut open the basic loops at the bottom of the loops and twist all 3 wires together for 1½″, very tightly, to make them as stiff as possible. Cut away all but ¾″ of the twisted wires, and do not tape. Trim off the top basic wires, leaving ¼″, and press the wire down the wrong side of the leaf, as usual.

Mark off the rows on the cone with a pencil or pen, following the pattern in Fig. 105. There are 7 rows of leaves, each row approximately 1¼″ above the preceding one. All leaves are spaced about ¾″.

The first 2 rows use 12 leaves; row 3 has 10 leaves; row 4, 9; row 5, 8; row 6, 6; and row 7, 4 leaves.

Attach the leaves, one at a time, starting at the bottom row. Insert the twisted wire stems into the styrofoam cone as far as they will go. Screw them, using a counterclockwise twist (to the left), then press the leaves flat against the cone, point end down. Insert the 12 leaves for row 2 in the same manner, 1¼″ above the first row, ¾″ apart, but between the leaves of the 1st row so that the points of the leaves of the 2nd row fill in the spaces between the tops of the leaves that are on the 1st row. They should overlap slightly. Add the remaining rows of leaves in the same way, and trim the tree to please your fancy.

This tree has a plastic stand and a "Jingle Bells" music box that rotates as it plays. However, a heavy stem wire can be inserted into the bottom of the cone, and the tree can be potted in a small saucer or clay pot filled with clay, then covered with glitter. The skirt shown is a 6″ felt circle that has been trimmed with cutouts from gold paper doilies.

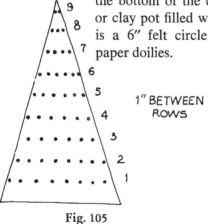

1″ BETWEEN
ROWS

Fig. 105

Disc, 1½" in diameter.
Icicles, 3" long.
See also color plate 22.

CHRISTMAS TREE TRIMMINGS

The large 4-foot-high tree shown at the left of the holiday buffet table has been decorated with beaded candy canes, large and small snowflakes, and light reflectors for each tiny light bulb. A few red bugle-bead discs and some silver icicles were also added for extra glitter.

The round discs have a basic of ½" with 17 rows in all. Make 2 for each disc and stack 2 of them right sides back to back, then twist the 2 top wires together for ½". Cut away all but ¼" and flatten it down the wrong side of one disc. Separate the discs at the bottom, cup each disc deeply with your thumb, in the center of the wrong side. Bring the bottom wires of both discs together so that the wrong sides face inward, and twist both sets of wires together. Use the twisted wires as a hook to attach the disc to a tree branch.

The icicles are 6" of silver bugle beads made into a narrow loop, then the 2 rows of beads are twisted and spiraled. Use the twisted wires as a hook. If you want a fatter icicle, use the same measurement, but give the narrow loop of beads a 4-row crossover, then twist and spiral the 4 rows of beads.

20" x 1". See also color plate 22.

HOLIDAY SWAG

This sparkling beaded wreath will add a warm welcome to any front door or fireplace during the holiday season. It is made by combining 12 small pine cones, 3 large pine cones, 1 small and 2 medium poinsettias, 10 clusters of red holly berries, with 4 small holly leaves to each cluster, and 26 large, shaded holly leaves (2 groupings with 4 leaves each, and 6 groupings with 3 leaves each). All of these

185

have been added onto a preshaped frame made with 2 pieces of taped 16-gauge wires, each piece 24″ long.

Shape the 16-gauge wires as in Fig. 106. These two wires will be trimmed separately, then combined. All of the patterns for the ingredients are listed in the index, except the poinsettia which can be found in my first book, *The Art of Making Bead Flowers and Bouquets*.

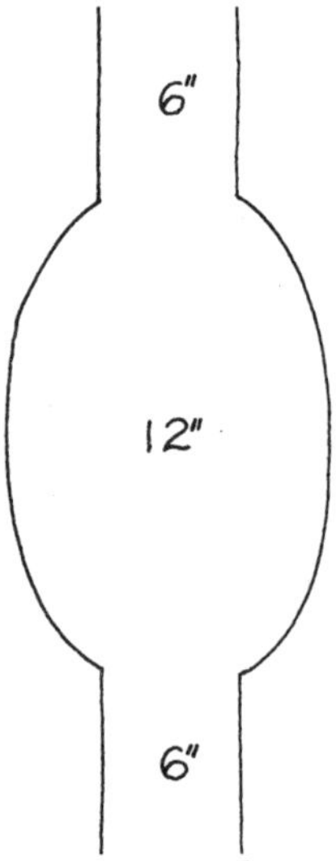

6″

12″

6″

Fig. 106

Large Holly Leaves

To the top of a 7- or 8-inch piece of taped 18- or 19-gauge stem wire, tape 4 leaves, allowing ½″ of stem on each leaf. Repeat on another stem wire. Tape 6 more wires, the same length, and to the top of each, tape on 3 leaves, allowing ½″ of stem on each leaf. Make 26, shaded.

Small Holly Leaves

This leaf is the same as the pattern used to trim the Holly Berry Bobeche. Make 21. Fig. 108.

Plain Leaves

BASIC: 1″, pointed tops, round bottoms, 13 rows.

Add 4 leaves to each small pine cone. Tape them 1″ below the base of each cone. Make 40.

Holly Berry Cluster

Use large red beads. Make 10 clusters. String the red berries on 26- or 28-gauge green painted spool wire, and 3″ from the open end of the wire group 3 red beads together by twisting both wires together for ½″. One-half inch from the twisted wires, group 3 more red beads together, and twist the wires together for ¼″. Continue until 10 groups of 3 beads each have been made. Allow 3″ of bare spool wire and cut the wire from the spool. Fig. 107. Join both end wires and twist. This makes 1 cluster. To the top of a 7″ piece of taped 18-gauge stem wire, tape 2 berry clusters and 4 small holly leaves. Make 3 more groupings in the same way. Make 2 more groupings, this time using 1 holly berry cluster and 4 leaves for each.

Poinsettias

Mount the flowers on taped 16-gauge wires, and one inch below the

Fig. 107

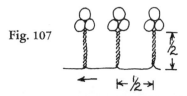

base of each of the 3 flowers, tape 4 poinsettia leaves around the stem wire.

Assembly of Swag

To the wire for the left half of the swag, tape in the following order: 1 grouping of 4 large, shaded holly leaves, 1 small pine cone with its 4 large leaves, 1 double cluster of holly berries with its leaves, 1 small pine cone with 4 leaves, 1 grouping of 3 large, shaded holly leaves, 1 double cluster of holly berries, 1 small pine cone with its 4 leaves, 1 medium poinsettia with 4 poinsettia leaves, 1 grouping of 3 large shaded holly leaves, 1 single cluster of holly berries, 2 small pine cones with 4 leaves each, 1 small poinsettia with 4 poinsettia leaves, and the other grouping of 4 large shaded holly leaves.

To the wire for the right side of the frame, start with 1 small pine cone and 4 large leaves, then continue in the same order as for the left side, finishing with 2 small pine cone groupings each with 4 leaves.

Combine the two halves of the frame by taping together the two 6″ of straight wire at the top and the bottom. Use the 2 top wires as a hook, and bend the bottom ones to one side, following the curve of the frame so that it will be hidden.

Large Pine Cones

Tape the 3 large cones to a 12″ piece of 18-gauge wire, spacing the cones about 1½ to 2 inches apart. Place it in the center of the swag and hook one end of the wire over the top of the frame. Secure with tape.

Tall bobeche, 6″ high, 2½″ wide at base. See also color plate 22.

HOLLY BERRY BOBECHE

Holly berries are a bright and cheery addition to any decorations for a festive holiday look. Accent a buffet table with holly berry accessories as shown in Color Plate 22.

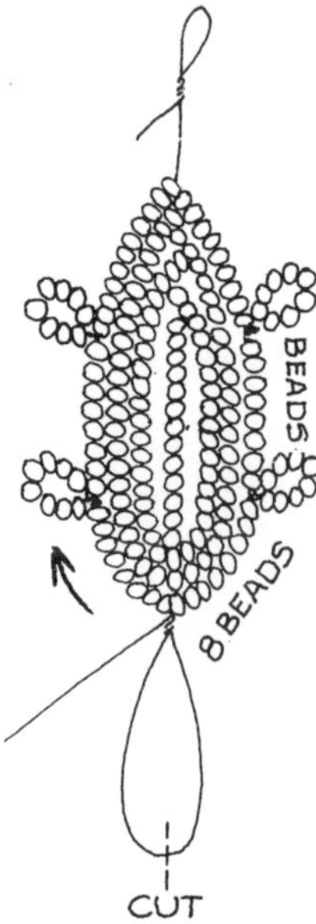

8 BEADS

8 BEADS

CUT

Fig. 108

Materials for one pair candle bobeches

Beads: 6 strands green; 126 large red holly berry (wooden or opaque) about ¼″ diameter.

Wires: 26- or 28-gauge green spool; two 30″ pieces 16-gauge.

If green spool wire isn't available to you, florists usually have cut green wires, 28- or 30-gauge, and they are usually cut to 18″, which is long enough to work with.

Berries

Two inches from the open end of the wire, group 3 red berries together and twist the wires together for ½″. Leave a ½″ space, group 3 more red beads together, and twist the wires together for ½″. Leave a ½″ space, group 3 more red beads together and twist the wires together for ½″. Allow 2″ of bare wire, and cut the wire from the spool. Twist the 2 end wires together to form a stem. Make 2 more sprigs in the same way, and group the 3 of them together by twisting 3 sets of wires together. Cover the combined wires with tape. Each bobeche has 7 of these groupings of 3 sets each. Fig. 107. Make 21 sets in all.

Leaves

Give the leaf a basic of ¾″ and 5 rows, with a pointed top and a round bottom. Rows 6 and 7 each have two 8-bead loops separated by 8 beads. To create the 6th row, push 8 beads to the base of the leaf, make an 8-bead loop, push 8 beads to the base of the 8-bead loop, and make a second 8-bead loop. Fig. 108. Complete the top portion of the 6th row, and the top portion of the 7th row. Directly opposite the 2nd 8-bead loop on the 6th row, make another 8-bead loop. Push 8 beads to the base of this 3rd 8-bead loop, and at the opposite end of the 8 beads, make another 8-bead loop, then finish off the bottom portion of the 7th row, twist the bottom wires together, cut the spool wire, and tape the bottom wires of the leaf. Make 12 for each bobeche, in green on green wire.

Assembly

To make the frame, tape a 30″ piece of 16-gauge stem wire, and coil it around a small glass jar or wooden dowel that measures approximately 1½″ in diameter. Stretch the 2 top coils of the wire to elongate them, and tape the bottom coils together to form a bottom rim.

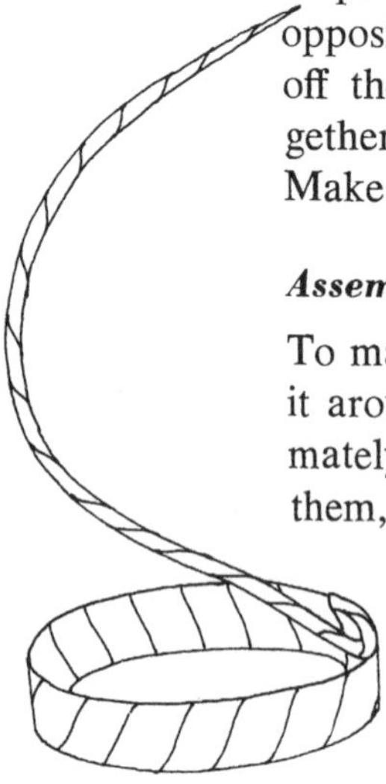

Fig. 109

Fig. 110

Fig. 109. Starting at the top of the frame, tape on 1 cluster of berries, 2 leaves opposite each other, 1 cluster of berries, 2 leaves, etc. until all leaves and berry clusters have been added. The stretched section of the frame should have 9 leaves and 4 clusters of berries. The bottom ring should have the remaining leaves and clusters alternating around the base.

1″ x ½″. See also color plate 22.

HOLLY BERRY CANAPE PICKS

Use the extra length picks for these. They are obtainable 3½ to 4 inches long and can be found in red and green during the holiday season. Use either red or green tape for assembly, depending on the color pick used.

Make one cluster of holly berries and two small holly leaves, using the same count as for the holly berry corsage, and tape them to the tops of the picks. Use them for hot or cold hors d'oeuvres for an extra touch of holiday glamor. Figs. 110, 112.

1½″ x 1½″. See also color plate 22.

HOLLY BERRY CIGARETTE HOLDER

These holders can serve more than one purpose. If they are to be used as cigarette containers, or to hold mustard or canapé picks, set a shot glass in the center as a liner. Without the liner, they may be used as candle bobeches.

Materials for one

Beads: 9 strands green for leaves; approximately 162 red holly berries. Wires: 28- or 30-gauge green spool; one 30″ piece 16-gauge.

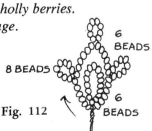

8 BEADS

6 BEADS

6 BEADS

Fig. 112

Leaves

BASIC: 1¼″, pointed tops, round bottoms, 13 rows.

Tape the stem wires on the leaves, and lace all 6 leaves together, through the center, right sides up. To close, join the end lacing wires, twist them for ½″, cut away all but ¼″, and tuck the remaining ¼″ of twisted wire to the inside. Cut off all but 1″ of stem on each leaf. Make 6.

Berry Clusters

Make 6 clusters of 3 units each, the same as for the spiral bobeche. Fig. 107.

Frame

Tape the 30″ piece of 16-gauge wire, and coil it around a 1½″ wooden dowel or glass jar. Tape the coils together. To the outside of the frame, tape on the 6 large leaves, halfway down the frame. Bend the leaf stems at right angles around the frame as you tape them on. In between each leaf tape on a cluster of red berries.

Leaf, 2⅝″ x 1¾″.
See also color plate 22.

HOLLY LEAVES (Shaded—Large)

The holiday swag as seen in Color Plate 22 shows holly leaves in 3 colors, dark green, light green, and white, as well as solid green ones. The greens are all transparent, and the white beads are opaline, although white alabaster or opaque can also be used.

Materials for one leaf

Beads: approximately 12″ dark green, 11″ medium green, 10″ white. Wire: 26-gauge spool

Leaf

BASIC: 1″, pointed top, round bottom, 11 rows.

Work the basic row and rows 2, 3, 4, and 5 in dark green. Allow 20" of bare spool wire, and cut the wire from the spool. Onto the 20" of bare wire, feed on enough light green to work rows 6, 7, 8 and 9. Feed on enough white beads to work rows 10 and 11. To execute these last 2 rows, count off 12 beads and push them to the base of the leaf. At the opposite end of the 12 beads, make a 12-bead loop. Push 15 beads to the base of the 12-bead loop, and make another 12-bead loop. Finish the top of rows 10 and 11 with beads, make a 12-bead loop opposite the second 12-bead loop on the 10th row, push 15 beads to the base of the 12-bead loop, make a 4th 12-bead loop opposite the 1st 12-bead loop and finish off the bottom of the 11th row. Fig. 113. Twist the bottom wires together to form a stem, and tape them. Shape the loops upward.

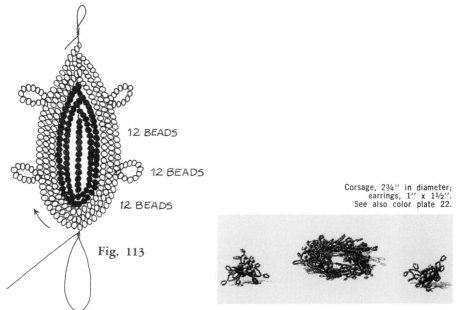

12 BEADS

12 BEADS

12 BEADS

Corsage, 2¾" in diameter; earrings, 1" x 1½". See also color plate 22.

Fig. 113

HOLLY BERRY CORSAGE AND EARRINGS

For the corsage, there are 20 leaves and 10 clusters of holly berries that have 3 berries each. They are taped to a frame made of 4 pieces of 28-gauge wire, each piece 7" long, twisted together, side by side, to give the frame body.

Materials

Beads: 2 strands red berry (¼" wide); 4 strands dark green

Wire: 28-gauge green spool
One bar pin

Leaves

Two inches from the open end of the beaded spool wire form a narrow loop with 12 beads, and close the loop by crossing the bottom wires twice, tightly, close to the base of the loop. Push 6 beads close to the base of the beaded loop. Close to the opposite end of the 6 beads, make an 8-bead loop. Push 6 beads close to the base of the 8-bead loop, and at the opposite end of the 6 beads, make another 8 bead loop. Continue until there are three 8-bead loops separated by 6 beads at the beginning and at the end. Fig. 112. Wrap this row of loops around the outside rim of the original 12-bead loop, wrap bare spool wire once around the bottom wire, allow 2″ of bare spool wire and cut the wire from the spool. Make 20, in green, on green wire.

Berries

Transfer a strand of the large red beads on the 28-gauge green wire, move 3 berries to within 2″ of the open end, form the 3 berries into a circle, and twist the two end wires together to form a stem. Fig. 109. Make 10 clusters.

Assembly of Corsage

One inch from the end of the taped frame wires, tape on a berry cluster and 2 leaves, another berry cluster and 2 leaves, until all have been added. Space them so that there is another inch of frame wire at the opposite end. Form the frame into a circle and intertwine the ends of the frame between the berries and leaves to secure the circle. Attach a bar pin on the underside of the wreath with short pieces of the green wire, twist and cut away excess.

Earrings

Make 1 berry cluster and 2 leaves, but this time make the two leaves continuously, so as to eliminate 1 set of wires. To do this, make the first leaf, and directly next to it make another 12-bead loop, 6 beads, 8-bead loop, 6 beads, 8 bead loop, etc., and twist the two wires together. Fig. 111.

Combine the berry cluster and the 2 leaves, twist all wires together for ¼″, and cut away all but one of the wires. Choose the longest

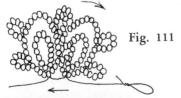

Fig. 111

wire to leave on. Use an earring frame that has a perforated
disc, and insert the long wire into the center hole, bring the long
wire up through another hole, then wrap the one wire around the
base of the combined berry and leaf wires 3 or 4 times to secure.
Cut away the excess close to the base of the cluster. Repeat for the
second earring.

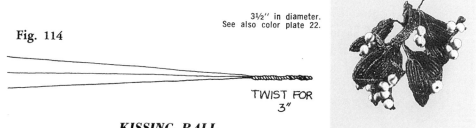

Fig. 114

3½" in diameter.
See also color plate 22.

TWIST FOR
3"

KISSING BALL

The ball shown is made with ¼" gold bugle beads, but beads of any
color can be used and they need not be bugles. The 11° round or
faceted beads work up just as well. The bugles, however, have more
glitter and are available in silver, red, blue, and green, as well as
gold.

Materials

Beads: 8 strands
Wire: 26-gauge gold spool

Cut 24 pieces of 26-gauge gold spool wire 14" long. Make 8
groupings of 3 wires each, by stacking 3 wires so that they are even
at the bottom (fig. 114) and twisting the 3 wires together for 3". Repeat 7 more times with the remaining 21 wires. Onto the open ends
of each wire in each of the 8 groups of 3 wires, transfer 6" of beads.
Crimp the open ends of the individual wires so that the beads won't
slip off. In each group of 3 wires, push the 6" of beads down to the
twisted wires, and twist together the 3 wires at the opposite end of
the 6" of beads, then spiral the 3 rows of beads, tightly. Fig. 115.
Either open up, or cut away the crimped ends of the wires. Gather
one end of all 8 units and twist the twisted wires together close to
the beads. Then twist together the twisted wires at the opposite end
of the beads.

Bring both ends of the twisted wires together so that the beaded
wires form a half circle. Overlap the twisted wires so that they

TWIST

Fig. 115

|← 3" →|

measure approximately 4″. Tape the wires together in the center and to these taped wires tape a cluster of mistletoe or holly berries. When the cluster of berries has been firmly attached, swing each beaded rib so that they form a ball. To the top of the ball attach either gold wire or red or green ribbon, so that the kissing ball may be hung in an archway or under a chandelier.

3½″ x 3½″.

MISTLETOE

This is the cluster for the kissing ball. It's quick and easy to make and is a fun addition to your permanent holiday decorations.

Materials

Beads: 1 bunch green; 24 six-millimeter white opaque beads (about ½″ diameter); 24 small black
Wire: 26-gauge gold

Leaves

Small. BASIC: 1¼″, pointed tops, round bottoms, 5 rows. Make 12, in green.
Large. BASIC: 1″, pointed tops, round bottoms, 7 rows. Make 12, in green.

Work all leaves with a generous basic loop—10 to 12 inches in each loop.

Combine the leaves in pairs, small leaves with small leaves, and large with large, by putting 2 together at a time, right sides facing in, and twisting the basic wires together to form stems. Bend the top half of each pair outward.

Berries

Cut 12 pieces of 26-gauge gold spool wire 12″ long. Put one small black bead in the center of each one, bring the ends of the wires together and insert both wires into 1 large white bead. Push the white

1   2   3   4

bead close to the black bead, separate the two wires, and onto each one place 1 small black bead and 1 white bead. Fig. 116. Bring the 2 wires together and twist them all the way to the end. Add a cluster of 3 berries in between each pair of leaves, allowing 2½" of stems on the clusters for the large pairs of leaves, and 1½" for the small pairs. Make 12 clusters.

Form all 12 clusters and their leaves into one bunch to form a ball of berries and leaves. Tape all the stems together. Attach, with tape, to the center wires of the kissing ball and arrange the cluster of berries and leaves around the center wires of the kissing ball frame.

Fig. 116

Small cone, 3" x 1".
See also color plate 22.

PINE CONES (*Small—Pinaceae*)

Each species of pine tree has its own particular kind of cone. The pattern that follows was designed from the cone of the white pine tree, and the cone consists of a central stem around which are arranged a series of overlapping scales (loop units). They have been used in the Holiday Swag shown in Color Plate 22.

Materials for one cone

Beads: 6 strands light or medium brown beads
Wires: 28-gauge spool; one 8" piece of 16- or 18-gauge for stem
Tape: Brown or twig

All units are made with continuous wraparound loops. Leave 1½" of bare spool wire at both ends of each unit.

Unit 1. Make 3 continuous narrow loop of beads, measuring ½" of beads for each loop. Each loop is wrapped around, once, with a row of beads as it is made. Make 1.

Unit 2. Make 4 continuous narrow loops of beads, measuring ¾" of beads for each loop. As each loop is completed, wrap around it once, with a row of beads. Make 1.

Unit 3. Make 4 continuous narrow loops, measuring 1" of beads for each loop. As each loop is made, wrap around once, with a row of beads. Make 2.

Unit 4. Make 5 continuous, narrow loops, measuring 1" of beads for each loop. As each loop is completed, wrap once around each loop with a row of beads. Make 4.

Unit 5. Make 5 continuous narrow loops, measuring ½" of beads for each loop. As each loop is completed, wrap once around each loop with a row of beads. Make 1.

Assembly

Tape the 8" piece of stem wire, and to the top of it, tape on 1 Unit 1. Tape down the stem for ½" and cut away the excess wires from Unit 1. Fit Unit 2 around the stem, ½" below the base of Unit 1. Tape for ½", and cut away the excess wires of Unit 2. Add the 2 parts of Unit 3, and 4 parts of Unit 4, and the 1 Unit 5 in the same way, setting each unit ½" lower than the previously added ones, and clipping away the excess wires of each part before adding the new ones. This will keep the stem slim. When the last unit has been taped on, continue taping to the end of the stem wire, and crush all units upward toward the top.

Large cone, 3" x 2½".
See also color plate 22.

PINE CONES (*Large*)

These plump cones with the tips of their scales touched with white pine resin are shown in the center of the Holiday Swag. Color Plate 22. Add them to a Christmas tree for an extra bit of realism.

Materials for one cone

Beads: 1½ bunches brown; ¼ bunch white alabaster or opaline
Wires: 28-gauge spool; 18-gauge for stem
Tape: Brown or twig

Cone

Unit 1. Prestring ½" of brown beads, ½" of white beads, 1" of brown beads, ½" of white, and ½" of brown. With ½" of brown, ½" of white and ½" of white make a narrow loop. Allow 1" of spool wire at both ends of the loop, twist both wires together to form a stem, cut the wire from the spool, and cover the twisted wires with tape. Repeat for a second loop using the remaining strung beads.

Unit 2. String beads as for Unit 1 and make a four-row crossover loop, measuring 1½" of beads for the initial loop. This will make one Unit 2. Repeat the stringing and make 1 more.

Unit 3. BASIC: 5 beads, round tops, pointed bottoms, 7 rows. Transfer several strands of brown beads to the spool wire and work the first 5¾ rows. Allow 5" of bare spool wire and cut the wire from the spool. Onto the open end of the 5" of bare wire put enough white beads to finish the 6th row and make the first ¼ of the 7th row, then add enough brown beads to finish the 7th row. Reduce the bottom wires to 2, twist and tape the wires, cut off top wire, leaving the usual ¼" and bend it down the wrong side of the petal. Make 10.

Unit 4. BASIC: 5 beads, round tops, pointed bottoms, 9 rows. Work the first 7¾ rows in brown, tip in white as for the petals in Unit 3, reduce bottom wires to 2, twist and tape, and remove all but ¼" of the top basic wire, as usual. Make 20, and tape the stems on all.

Assembly

Tape a 7" piece of 18-gauge stem wire, and to the top, tape the 2 loops of Unit 1 and the 2 crossover loops of Unit 2. Tape down the stem for ¼", and around the stem add 4 of Unit 3, right sides facing up. Tape down another ¼" and around the stem add 6 of Unit 3. Add 4 layers of Unit 4, 5 petals to each layer, spacing these 4 layers ¼" apart down the stem. Tape to the bottom of the stem. Arch each petal out and down to shape.

VI DESIGNS FOR BRIDES

12" x 7".
See also color plate 4.

BRIDAL BOUQUET #1
(Daisies, Lily-of-the-valley, and Baby's-breath)

The flowers used in this bridal bouquet comprise patterns that have already been described in *The Art of Making Bead Flowers and Bouquets*, but because of the exceptionally large number of requests for details about it, I'm including them here.

Materials for one bouquet

Beads: 5 bunches for flowers; 1½ bunches for leaves and stamens
Wires: 26-gauge gold spool; 16-gauge for stem
White tape

There are 18 crossover daisies in white alabaster, using 2" of beads for the initial loop of beads before the crossover. Each daisy has a beehive center with 10 rows and one anemone leaf. Both the beehive and center have been worked in the real gold beads. There are 7 sprigs of lily-of-the-valley, and 7 sprigs of baby's breath with 5 units each. Gold 26-gauge wire was used throughout, and very long wires were left on all units. Everything was mounted to the top of a 7" piece of 16-gauge wire using white tape. This 16-gauge wire formed the handle, that was covered with white satin ribbon when the bouquet was completed.

White pearl beads can be used in place of the white alabaster beads if desired. Both beads are a soft white.

10″ x 6″. See also color plate 4.

BRIDAL BOUQUET #2

This bouquet is made all in white pearl, with the exception of the gold baby's-breath and the stamens in the orchids. It consists of 2 orchids, 4 clusters of stephanotis, and 7 sprigs of baby's-breath. Both orchids are taped to a 9″ piece of 16-gauge wire. Using white tape, the stephanotis clusters were added under the orchids, and the baby's-breath was added across the top. The 16-gauge wire serves as a handle. Wrap it with narrow white satin ribbon and sew it at the open end to secure.

8¼″ x 4″. See also color plate 4.

BIBLE BOUQUET

For the bride who wishes to carry something small, trim a white bible or prayer book with one pearl orchid and satin ribbon streamers with orange blossoms tacked to the ends of the ribbons. Make the orange blossoms the same as for the large flower on the bridal crown. Small rose buds or daisies would be just as effective. The ribbons have been taped to the stem of the orchid and the combined bouquet has been sewn to a band of wider satin ribbon made to fit over the front cover of the book.

STEPHANOTIS (*Madagascar-Jasmine*)

One of the most frequently used flowers in bridal bouquets, the stephanotis is soft and waxy in appearance, and falls gracefully in cascades. It is shown in Color Plate 4 in a bridal bouquet combined with baby's-breath and orchids. White pearl or white alabaster beads are a wise choice because of their mellow, not stark, whiteness.

Materials for fifteen flowers and fifteen buds

Beads: 2 bunches white pearl
Wire: 26-gauge gold spool

Flower

Crimp the open end of the beaded spool wire, and move 1″ of beads to the crimped end. Three inches from the crimped end, make 3 continuous four-row crossover loops, using 12 beads for the initial loop. Bring down 1″ of beads to the bottom of the first 1″ of beads and wrap spool wire one and a half times around the wire at the base of the first 1″ of beads. Bead up the left side of the 2 rows of beads, bring bare spool wire between the 2nd and 3rd loops, and cross the bare wire to the left of the 3rd loop. Make 2 more 4-row crossover loops, the same size as the first 3, bead down to the bottom of the three 1″ rows of beads, twist the bottom wires together, allow 3″ of bare spool wire, and cut the wire from the spool. Fig. 117. Make 15, in white pearl.

Fig. 117

Bud

The bud is made the same way as the flower, except that it has only 2 loops of 12 beads each and they are a 3-row crossover. Crimp the open end of the beaded spool wire, move 1″ of beads to the crimped end of the wire, and 3″ from the crimped end, make 2 3-row crossover loops, and bead to the bottom of the first 1″ of beads.

Twist the bottom wires together to form a stem. Fig. 118. Make 15, in white pearl.

Calyx

Make 4 continuous 12 bead loops, allowing 3″ of bare wire at both ends. Make 30, in white pearl.

Assembly of Flowers and Buds

Set one calyx at the base of each flower and bud, and twist both sets of wires together to form stems.

Assembly of Clusters

Group 5 flowers and 5 buds together to form one cluster, by twisting the stems together, tightly. Repeat for 2 more clusters. If the clusters are to be used in an arrangement with other flowers, mount the clusters on 16-gauge wire. If they are to be used as part of a bridal bouquet, they need not be mounted separately, but will be added to the handle of the bouquet.

Fig. 118

4½″ x 4″. See also color plate 4.

ORCHID

There are many varieties in the orchid family, small, large, fringed, etc. This one, done in white pearl beads, has a waxy appearance and is particularly attractive when combined with the stephanotis in the bridal bouquet described at the beginning of this chapter. It may be made in all white, or the small center petal may be done in a soft pastel. Real gold beads were used in the bridal bouquet.

Materials

Beads: 9 strands pearl; 1 strand gold
Wire: 26-gauge gold or silver

Throat Petal

BASIC: 5 beads, round top, pointed bottom, 19 rows. Lace the throat petal once, through the middle, right side up. Cup the petal and roll back the top of it. Fold the petal in half, lengthwise, twist the lacing wires together for ½", cut away all but ¼", and tuck the wires into the center of the petal, pressing it flat against the beads. Make 1.

Large Petal

BASIC: ½", round top, pointed bottom, 19 rows. Make 2.

Center Petal

BASIC: 4 beads, round top, pointed bottom, 11 rows. Make 1, in gold.

Small Petal

BASIC: 1¾", pointed top, round bottom, 9 rows. Reduce to 2 the bottom wires on all petals. Make 3.

Assembly of Flower

Roll the center petal, wrong side in, and insert into the middle of the throat petal. Twist both sets of wires together.

To the base of the throat petal, attach a piece of 32-gauge assembly wire, wrapping it 2 or 3 times to secure. Add the 2 large petals across the back of the throat petal, right sides up, and wrap assembly wire twice, tightly, with each addition. Between the 2 large petals add one small one, right side up, and where the throat petal is closed, add the 2 remaining small petals, right sides up. After the last petal has been added, wrap assembly wire around the base of the flower 3 or 4 times more, to secure, and cut away the excess. Cover the bottom wires with tape, and shape the petals, up and out. Curve the 2 small petals out at the base of the throat.

3½" high. See also color plate 4.

BRIDAL CROWN

Created especially for one of my students some time ago, the idea has started a deluge of requests from others. Some have been made and used, others have been completed and "put away" until daughter's Wedding Day.

Materials

Beads: Approximately 3 bunches white pearl beads
Wires: 26-gauge gold spool; 30- or 32-gauge for assembling; 18-gauge for stem
White tape

The frame consists of six 18-gauge wires that have been covered in white tape. The wires are 14" long, two have been wrapped with pearl beads for 12" (leaving 1" at each end without beading), two wires have been beaded for 11", and two for 10". There are 2 sets of wires that have been joined together, one on top of the other, by wrapping lacing wires between the rows of beads. One set uses one wire that has been beaded for 12" and one wire that has been beaded for 11". The other set uses one wire that has been beaded for 11" and one that has been beaded for 10". This uses four of the beaded wires, and they have been placed between the top single beaded wire and the bottom single beaded wire. The top wire has 10" of beading, and the bottom one has 12" of beading. This allows the crown to become slightly narrower at the top. All 6 beaded wires are joined together, one on top of the other, with pearl beads that have been strung on 26-gauge gold wire to keep the beaded wires separate and to give the entire crown a lattice effect. Each row of beaded wires is about 1" apart. Fig. 119.

The "frame" has been trimmed with 7 large flowers and 28 small flowers. The large flower is a 5-petal continuous wraparound, and the initial loop on each petal is 15 beads. Each large flower has 2 leaves, each with a basic of 5 beads with 5 rows, pointed tops and

203

round bottoms. The small flower has 5 continuous loops with 10 beads to each loop. There are 14 groupings of 2 small flowers with 2 small leaves to each. The small leaf is a basic of 5 beads with 3 rows, pointed tops and round bottoms. Add the pairs of leaves to the flowers by twisting their stems close to the base of the flowers, then twisting flower and leaf wires together for ½". All flowers have been secured to the frame with gold spool wire, after cutting the flower stems short and covering them with white tape. The end wires of the frame have been left exposed so that the lace or tulle veil may be attached.

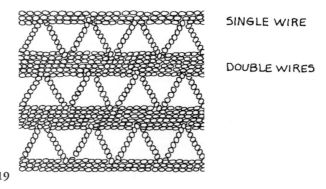

SINGLE WIRE

DOUBLE WIRES

Fig. 119

VII MAKING A BEAD FLOWER ARRANGEMENT

1. You will need from 2 to 10 pounds of non-hardening floral clay. Warm it first by working it in your hands (or setting it in the sun). Pack the container of your choice with clay, then add a sturdy mound in the center. All stems will be inserted in this mound, so be sure to make it big enough. Cover all exposed clay with florist sheet moss, green side up. (*If you are using a glass container,* line it first with sheet moss, green side down, then add the clay and top with sheet moss, green side up.)

2. Use tall spikes or stems with small buds to make the framework or outline. Use big round solid flowers in the brightest colors, or clusters of smaller flowers wired together to form one large unit, as the center of interest (usually where the vertical of the arrangement crosses the neck of the container). Use small light airy flowers or leaves as fillers or as trailing vines.

3. Every stem should vary in height. Usually the outline stems are the tallest or widest ones; the center-of-interest flowers are on the shortest stems. Use heavy shears to cut off the stems if necessary. To lengthen stems, wire them to pieces of wire coat hangers cut with heavy wire cutters, then conceal joining with floral tape.

4. Wire, flowers and leaves in small natural groupings or branches so you have fewer stems to work with. Insert the groupings into the central mound of clay so that all seems to grow from one trunk.

5. Give depth to your arrangement by facing flowers and leaves left, right, and profile; not all lined up like so many soldiers. You can open the flowers by flattening them gently, or close them by compressing the petals, so they simulate different stages of maturity. See design and technique pointers given under *Descriptions of the Color Plates.*

DESCRIPTIONS OF THE COLOR PLATES

1. Boudoir lamps (description in text).

2. Left to right: two branches of Royal Crown flowers with a branch of yellow mimosa; 17½" x 7". Four branches of blue petunias flanking a branch of yellow tansy; 11½" x 7". Six calla lilies; 16" x 10".

3. Three white foxgloves right, left, and center, form the outline for this bouquet. Next, three spoon mums were used to create the

center mass, and the smaller spray flowers (three lady bells, ten freesia), were added as fillers. 19" x 27".

4. An all-white wedding assortment consisting of a bridal crown and three bouquets: two orchids, stephanotis and baby's breath; twenty-four daisies and five lily-of-the-valley; a Bible bouquet with an orchid and seven orange blossoms.

5. A heavy tube of cardboard from a bolt of fabric (it must be cut to fit firmly into the container) has been stuffed with modeling clay, covered with moss, and wedged into an amethyst crystal vase. It holds an assortment of chrysanthemums (three spider, three button, three cushion, one two-flower spray and a single), four star-of-Bethlehem and a spray of meadow rue. 29" x 18".

6. Three bunches of grapes are arranged with foliage. 13½" x 14".

7. (Cover) An arrangement of five anthurium and two birds of paradise set among five hosta leaves. 20" x 12½".

8. The arrangement begins with a bunch of shrimp flowers on the left side of the bamboo container, with shorter bunches added to the left (there are four branches in all) and to the right. Five hibiscus are grouped in a low central position, and three palmetto leaves fill in at the left and bottom, with a single shrimp flower as a finale. 17½" x 19".

9. Wedding cake in a white bisque bowl. First, the lowest row: twenty clusters of wild flowers. Then, just above a layer of eighteen clusters of wild pansies (see "The Art of Making Bead Flowers and Bouquets," p. 107), followed by a third row, slightly higher, of sixteen clusters of orange arum. The stems of the five clusters of snowflakes were taped together and inserted in the center, at the top. The pyramid effect was achieved by varying the length of the stems of each layer.

10. Twenty-four long-stemmed tea roses in two shades of pink, with four maidenhair fern, nine large sprigs of baby's breath. 27" x 17".

11. This red, white and blue bouquet is comprised of five red peonies, one long and two short sprays of bridal wreath and nine blue cornflowers (bachelor buttons). The technique of forming the arrangement is similar to that used for plate 8.

12. Wisteria tree (70" x 50"), planted in a brass-bound bucket.

13. Picture frame, 25¼" x 21¼" x 4¼". *Left, top to bottom:* cup and saucer with calla lilies; white basket with strawberries; loop

basket with primroses. *Center:* trellis with bluebells. *Right, top to bottom:* cutting basket with trillium; hyacinth in beaded flower pot; beaded basket with arum.

14. Twenty-nine Boston fern are arranged in the lavabo container exactly as described above for plate 15. 23″ x 18″.

15. This hanging begonia is a front-sided plant only, with the longest-stemmed flowers placed close to the front and hanging over the edge of the container; all other flowers were added behind the first row, except for a few reserved for uprights across the back. The filler: extra clusters of loopy leaves or fern. 11½″ x 12½″.

16. Wrought iron spiral library steps (74″ x 20″) are adorned, top to bottom, with scales holding primroses and maidenhair fern; strawberry patch; crown imperial; Easter lily; hydrangea; giant iris.

17. A brilliant, forthright display of giant Matilija poppies, three each of red, orange and yellow. 39″ x 19″. The small brass goblet to the left contains three white mountain bluets and eight small red poppies; a sprig of bridal wreath lies at the right.

18. The white-and-yellow theme is first stated with a geometric triangle of three Ginny roses, then supplemented by five large carnations. Five sprigs of wisteria, five tritoma, five silver dollars and two yellow gentian complete the scene. 23½″ x 30″.

19. Five varied groupings of dried flowers, as follows: *Top shelf, left to right:* six wood roses, five ti leaves, six branches of bittersweet and three castor bean leaves arranged, again, according to the method described for plate 8; 15″ x 15″. Twelve peacock feathers and one football mum; 18″ x 18″. *Bottom shelf, left to right:* beetle box with three small tulips, four iris and a pair of wild flowers and thistles; 7½″ x 5½″. Antique basket with four clusters of sweet peas and sprigs of bluebells; 3″ x 2″. Large beaded basket with nine asters; 7″ x 8″.

20. Close-up of tree shown on plate 22.

21. Console lamps (description in text).

22. This Christmas buffet table is decked with a holiday swag; two holly bobeches, one tall, one short; holly pin and earrings; a beaded basket with holly; canapé picks; a kissing ball; three beaded trees. The artificial Scotch pine tree is trimmed with snowflakes, light reflectors, candy canes, discs, and icicles.

23. Ming tree (description in text).

INDEX